How to Awaken Your Inner Dragon
Visualizations to Empower Yourself and the World

by
JEN WARD

How to Awaken Your Inner Dragon
Copyright © 2018 Jen Ward
All rights reserved.
Cover Artwork by Jen Ward
Jenuine Healing®
ISBN-10: 0-9994954-4-5
ISBN-13: 978-0-9994954-4-5

There seems to be a desperate need for a place to bring questions of a Spiritual nature. It is surprising how many individuals feel so isolated because they are having certain experiences and have no means to figure out what is happening. I would like to say to them collectively, "You are not alone."

It is also said that in this day and age, it is harder to know whom to trust. Everyone seems to either have their own agenda, represent an agenda or be speaking from an egotistical point of view (however subtle that may be). I am not saying I have all the answers, but I can tell you what my "agenda" is. It is to walk my life's purpose by helping others discover their life's purpose.

It is a Joy for me to hear, "I have been struggling my whole life with this and now I have an answer."

So, feel free to think of me as a "Spiritual Dear Abby." I will do my best to answer as many of your questions as possible. By sending in your question, you may be helping many others who struggle with the same issue. At the very least, I am hoping that people realize that they aren't alone in their experience, that many others can relate and, in a way, we are in this together. In this outer world that is so stark sometimes, that in itself may be a great comfort.

I look forward to getting to know you and having you get to know me.

With Love and Appreciation for the journey you walk,

- Jen

CONTENTS

	Introduction	1
1	A Shortcut to Enlightenment	2
2	An Understanding of the Chakra System	4
3	Beyond Reiki	6
4	Chakra Clearing	7
5	Calibrate the Day	10
6	Dealing with These "Trying Times"	11
7	Healing the Chakra System	13
8	Developing Taps for Others	14
9	Self-Sabotage	15
10	Fighting Ourselves	16
11	When Feeling Sad, Angry or Moody	17
12	You Deserve Wellness	18
13	The Golden Globe Heart Chakra Technique	20
14	Triggers	22
15	If You Are Afraid of a Certain Experience	23
16	An Energetic Reason for Chronic Pain	24
17	Home Sickness	25
18	Embedded Souls	26
19	Alleviating Dis-ease	27
20	A Curse	29
21	The Energetic Significance of the "Heil Hitler" Salute	30
22	Shatter All Illusions	33

23	Technique for Heart Disease and High Blood Pressure	36
24	Antacid Healing Technique	37
25	Cursing	37
26	How to Rid Your Face of Wrinkles	38
27	Coping with Stress and Eating Disorders	39
28	Growing Old	42
29	Reverse the Aging Process	44
30	Healing Through Self-Awareness	45
31	Energetic Liposuction	47
32	Technique for Cellular Healing	48
33	Taps to Conceive a Healthy Baby	49
34	People Will Speak of Problems and Illnesses	51
35	Procedures	52
36	Removing Toxic Anger	53
37	Heal Your Heart	55
38	Sinus Issues	56
39	The Understanding of Physical Pain	57
40	Take in Gratitude	59
41	Take Out Pain	60
42	If You Feel The Pain of Others	61
43	Technique for Changing Your DNA	61
44	Synthetic Happiness	63
45	Technique to Counter Worry	65
46	Technique to Let Go of Issues	67
47	Things That Create Stress	68
48	Technique to Make Life Manageable	69
49	Tending to a Zen Garden	70
50	Healing Technique for the Planet	72

51	The Melting Crayon Technique	73
52	Beautiful Glowing Violet Ember of Love	73
53	Inner Beauty as a Reality	74
54	Why Waste a Song?	75
55	Releasing the Aversion to Color	76
56	Technique to Squeeze Out the Stagnant Energy	78
57	Give Yourself Permission	79
58	Technique for Conscious Living	79
59	Just Shift!	80
60	Technique to Break Down Your Issues	80
61	Saying Grace	81
62	Reactionary	82
63	Walking into Energy	83
64	How to Watch Television	84
65	How and Why to Emote	85
66	Technique to Center	86
67	The Ice Technique	87
68	Some Helpful SFT	87
69	The Reconnection Technique	88
70	Overcoming Rape	89
71	Technique to Love Yourself	91
72	When You Are in Pain and Panicking	91
73	Utilizing Self-Energy	92
74	Love Is as Permeating as the Warming Effects of the Sun	92
75	Technique to Satiate the Love Starved	93
76	Technique to Drop the Hate	93
77	Technique to Neutralize the "Enemy"	94
78	Love All from Within	95

#	Title	Page
79	How What We Think Affects Others	96
80	Our Best Work	98
81	Technique to Fill in the Void	99
82	Technique to Remove the Void	102
83	Suicidal Thoughts	103
84	Dying Too Soon	103
85	Technique to Love Those Who Have Crossed	104
86	The Gift of Survival	105
87	The Heart Light Technique	106
88	Stripping Down the Layers	107
89	Techniques to Overcome Limitations	108
90	Fear of Being Alone and Empty	109
91	Visualize the Love	110
92	Release the Effects of a Full Moon	111
93	The Dream Catcher – Lint Trap Technique	112
94	Speech Empowerment	113
95	Integrity	115
96	Misunderstanding God	117
97	The Tunnel to God Technique	118
98	Technique to Expand into Your God-Self	119
99	Healing Any Body Part	121
100	The Physiological Exchange of Emotional Energy	125
101	Raising Your Vibratory Rate	128
102	Nurturing Greatness	131
103	Angel Healing	132
104	Technique to Remedy Lumps in the Breasts	134
105	Bubble Technique	135
106	Contemplation Versus Meditation	136

107	The Practice of Responsible Thinking	137
108	Release Being One's Own Worst Enemy	139
109	Real Time Exchange on Negative Thoughts	141
110	How to Make Disease Accessible to All	142
111	The Pac Man Technique	145
112	Many of Us Are So Busy	146
113	Technique to Perpetuate Purity	147
114	Technique for Using White Sound	149
115	Sensitive Children	151
116	Technique to Compensate Yourself	153
117	Technique to Assist Sensitive Children	153
118	The Teenager Technique	154
119	How to Meet Santa Claus	155
120	Technique to "Fill Up" on Christmas	157
121	Ways to Heal Your Pet's Stress	158
122	When Pets Get Lost	160
123	Walking Technique	160
124	Trusting Your Instinct	161
125	What Is Possible Is Incredible!	162
126	Thread Yourself	162
127	Vitamin "Be"	163
128	Perpetual Contemplation	164
129	The Strength of Balance	166
130	Regaining Empowerment	167
131	Recognizing Your Own Empowerment	169
132	Technique to Challenge One's Own Beliefs	171
133	When Emptying Your DVR	172
134	Uncovering Our Own Past Lives	173

135	Technique to Unclutter Your Life	174
136	If the Laughter of Others Is Annoying	176
137	Sound Wheel Technique	176
138	Repairing Boundaries	177
139	Don't Fall for It!	178
140	A Question on Maintaining Boundaries	179
141	The Human Exhaust Technique	181
142	The Flasher Technique	182
143	Being Aligned and Balanced	183
144	Better Boundaries	184
145	Technique for When You Are Being Intruded Upon	186
146	Network of Love	187
147	Technique to Stay Humble	187
148	Technique for Hiring Someone to Help You	188
149	How to Stay Centered	188
150	We Wouldn't Let a Stranger Talk About Us	189
151	Bursting Bubbles of Illusion	189
152	New Starts	190
153	Empowerment Technique	191
154	Technique to Have a Love Affair with Yourself	191
155	The Automatic Sprinkler	192
156	Many of Us Are Empathic	193
157	The Sound Canceling Technique	194
158	Issues Don't Happen in a Vacuum	195
159	You 2.0	195
160	Empowered, Awakened and Enlightened	196
161	Breaking Down the Ego	198
162	Listen to Your Own Wisdom	199

163	Changing One's Life Cycle	200
164	Connecting	201
165	Love as Self-Responsibility	202
166	Hot Potato	203
167	Concede to Kindness	205
168	Empowerment Is Not Abusing Power	206
169	Discounting One's Life	207
170	Bliss After Murder	207
171	Death Is the New Birth	208
172	Real Time Assistance with Psychic Influences	210
173	Online Dating Scammers	212
174	Undoing Negative Posts	216
175	Who We Are	217
176	Don't Be a "Has Been"	218
177	You Know That Feeling of Just Needing to Complain?	220
178	Be Light as a Feather	220
179	Allow Your Atoms to Dance!	221
180	Babies	222
181	Alternative to Counting Sheep	222
182	Smiling with Your Energy	223
183	Why the Law of Attraction May Not Be Working for You	225
184	Actualizing Self-Love	227
185	Choosing Love	229
186	Problem Solving Technique	230
187	Technique to Cut the Drama	231
188	Stop Being a Know It All	232
189	Being Agreeable	233
190	Techniques to Right Past Transgressions	234

191	Confusing Anger for Strength	235
192	Technique for Someone Who Confronts You	236
193	Technique for Disarming Anger	237
194	Becoming a Toxic-Free Zone	239
195	Putting Personal Assaults into Perspective	240
196	Negate Negativity	241
197	Empowered in Friendship	242
198	Technique to Stretch Your Capacity for Compassion	244
199	The Fruit of Your Own Tree	245
200	The Frozen Tree Technique	246
201	Technique to Listen	247
202	Technique to Bring Others to Their Senses	248
203	Raise Your Vibration	249
204	Goodwill	250
205	Choose to Improve	250
206	How to Stay "In Love"	251
207	Breaking Up Gracefully	252
208	Divorce	254
209	Stop Feeling Like a Fifth Wheel	256
210	Changing Friend Dynamics	259
211	Being Popular	260
212	Craving or Avoiding Attention	262
213	Relationship Worksheet	263
214	See Your Interactions	267
215	Honing the Ho'oponopono Technique	267
216	Transcending	268
217	Mastering Direct Knowing	269
218	Vantage Point	270

219	Living Your Purpose	271
220	You Are the Center of Your World	272
221	How It Works	273
222	The Dynamics	274
223	Raising Our Vibration	275
224	Tapping Into Your Own Wisdom	278
225	How Awesome Is That?	279
226	How To Live Your Purpose	280
227	The Pipeline Technique	282
228	Guardian Technique	283
229	Technique to Hone Your Craft	283
230	Technique to Expand Your Energy	284
231	The Last Game of Candy Crush	285
232	The Super Bowl Technique	286
233	The Correlation Between Healing and Physics	287
234	The River Technique	290
235	Spiritual Activism – Technique to Untangle the World	292
236	Let's Dislodge a Logjam	293
237	Put an End to This Selfish Act	294
238	Technique to Turn Chaos into Celestial Music	295
239	How to Save the World	296
240	Shatter the Glass Ceiling Technique	298
241	The Power of Intention	300
242	Working with the Spiritual Law of Intention	301
243	Merry Christmas Right Now	305
244	Technique to Expand Your Consciousness	306
245	Knock First!	308
246	Technique to Heal the World	309

247	Technique to Love Yourself	310
248	Perpetuating Positivity	311
249	Loving Balance	313
250	Jen's Version of Ho'Oponopono	314
251	The Peanut Brittle Technique	315
252	The Extension of Your Own Face	316
253	Energetic Liposuction	318
254	Humans Are Living, Breathing, Portal Makers	319
255	Conscious Choice	320
256	The Social Media Technique	321
257	What to Tell Yourself	325
258	Leeches and Slugs	327
259	I Wish	328
260	Everything Matters	329
	About the Author	330
	Other Books by Jen Ward	332

HOW TO AWAKEN YOUR INNER DRAGON

INTRODUCTION

YOU ARE WHO YOU ARE

Either you know yourself to be a divine spark of God with freedom of choice or a breathing piece of matter that's a victim of circumstance. Decide who you are. If you are a victim of circumstance then everyone else is a victim of circumstance as well. We are all made of the same stuff. But if you see the greatness in others, you must recognize greatness in yourself. If you then recognize greatness in yourself by default, you must take ownership of it.

You must then acquaint yourself with all the amenities that being a divine Spark of God affords. You. Because being a victim in an empowered state of awareness is just too much of a transgression to reasonably tolerate. This is what so many of us are grappling with right now. We are learning the blueprints and instruction manuals of this empowered self.

To shrivel up and cower on a wind glider or to soar into the setting sun sniveling on one's knees is too ridiculous for any soul to wrestle with. Stand up and operate the equipment that you were equipped with. Don't you dare allow anyone to pull you around on a string or tow you to serve their own agenda. Operate under your own accord. Anything else is unworthy of the greatness of your capabilities.

1 A SHORTCUT TO ENLIGHTENMENT

I have found in my energy work that there are certain experiences that are Universal. Some of them are: the feeling of being isolated and unique to the point of not relating to others, the need to overcome physical, emotional and mental pain, and feeling special in a way that others cannot relate to. All experiences are valid and true. They seem to be milestones on the way to enlightenment.

I have also found that on the road to enlightenment, the individual sabotages the self. Truth is Universal. We believe we have to dig for truth but in our zeal, we cover ourselves with the same dirt that we cleared from the trenches. There is an easier way. Just embrace the simplicity of it. Be the Love. Ride Love like the music of a flute in the wind into the heart of truth.

We need to unhinge ourselves from all the trauma and experiences that we have accrued over lifetimes and just let them go. We identify too greatly with this little clump of flesh that we think we are. We are so much more than that little mound of physical matter. We are the ones that manifest our own greatness. We are the ones that walk in Heaven while still on earth if we dare. And we are the ones to empower ourselves to slough off the mediocrity of this world and live the life of both freedom and service to a greater good.

The purpose of life is to learn to give and receive Love in the most sublime ways. There is always another step in the capacity to Love. Each individual could do so much more to plug into the Universality of Love everyday by the thoughts they choose to edit and the choices they make moment to moment. If everyone chose simply to rise to the occasion and take themselves seriously as spiritual beings, this whole experience of existing on earth would be much different.

A starting point is to ask yourself every day, "What would Love do?" Before you say or even think any thought, ask yourself three things? "Is it true, necessary and kind?" Let that be the gauge to know whether to give life to another thought form. Turn your back on negativity of any kind as if it is a spoiled child. Dry up negativity and don't engage in fertilizing it with your attention. And suspend all judgment. For when you judge someone, you are in denial that you are the one that needs to focus on you. Judging someone else is a form of self-sabotage in your journey to truth.

2 AN UNDERSTANDING OF THE CHAKRA SYSTEM

If people understood the mechanism of chakras, maybe the concept of them wouldn't seem so strange. Some may know them as just little circles that are color coded to each area of the body. Maybe it doesn't make sense how wearing a color or focusing on a particular color can benefit one's health. So I thought I would share my understanding of chakras.

Have you ever seen how cotton candy is made? There is a huge circular tub with a large metal wand that distributes a fine fluff along the outer edge of the tub. This is the visual I use to understand how energy is collected and funneled into the body.

A chakra is an energy funnel that uses very subtle electromagnetic attraction to draw energy into the body and feed it to the glands where it can be processed for particular uses. Since the energy vortexes don't rely on gravity to funnel energy in, they can still work when they are on their side. So each chakra is made up of at least four funnels that draw energy into that particular area of the body.

Since Light comes in all colors, it makes sense that each color has a different quality to it or a different vibration. Each chakra attracts an energy of a different vibration. The root chakra, which is located at the base of the pubic bone, collects energy that has the vibration of the color red. This color has its own characteristics and benefits for the body. And so when someone senses your root chakra is not working, they will suggest you attract more energy to you that vibrates as red by thinking of or wearing red.

This happens for every chakra of the body. Many people think that there are only seven chakras. But I know there to be nine. There is a chakra above the head and one below the feet. These chakras are located where our energy field begins and are vital to feeding energy into the system, maintaining our boundaries and keeping us plugged into the Universe as an energetic system. All are vital parts of our health.

Since all bodily functions rely on the energy we receive from air, water and food, it isn't so far-fetched to realize that maintaining a healthy chakra system is vital to our health as well. And since energy follows thought, by visualizing the chakra system as operating properly, we can help detect glitches in our own energy system and repair them with our own loving intention.

Here is a technique: In contemplation, visualize these cone-like energy systems of your own body. Scan your body and get a sense of which ones may not be functioning well. Visualize fixing them by any visual that is helpful. Saturate them with the correlating color, imagine adjusting the cone or even visualize pulling out dark energy that may be plugging it up.

As you go through your day, pay attention to your chakras and tune into them to visualize them functioning well. Pay attention to what colors you are attracted to give yourself a clue as to what chakras are working well and which ones need some attention.

Then the next time you hear someone talk about chakras, you will have a working understanding of what they are trying to convey and it won't seem quite so abstract.

3 BEYOND REIKI

Reiki energy is a wonderful Universal tool. It is the life force collected and channeled by a facilitator to focus and channel energy. I use the analogy of a magnifying glass collecting sunlight to heat an object. That's my simplistic way to explain Reiki. The facilitator is acting as the magnifying glass to direct Universal Energy.

I have met people who said that they have tried to receive Reiki and it made them too agitated. I have my own understanding of why this happens. The people who can't tolerate Reiki, I believe, have too much pent up energy. They can't handle any more. They may need stagnant energy, which is caused by old emotional issues, released from their energy field. This is what I do for a client. I help their body release energy blockages so that their body can receive the healing benefits of Reiki.

This is easy enough to do. The facilitator holds their hands over the client's diaphragm, and instead of channeling energy in, they draw old energy out. I would recommend that the facilitator send the stagnant energy through their hands, away from themselves, and into a river of light. This is done with a visualization of the process and a simple intent.

Once the stagnant energy is released, the facilitator can close up the energy field. They can then begin the original intent of being a channel for the Reiki energy. I have found this to be a very effective way to bring ease to a body.

4 CHAKRA CLEARING

Chakras are energy systems in the body. They function by pulling energy into the body and feeding it to the glandular system where it is processed and distributed throughout the whole system. Some people can balance their systems by cleansing and empowering the chakras of the body.

There are nine chakras that work with the personal energy field and seven of them that are within the body itself. Each one of them is associated with a color and they are hopefully in alignment at the core of the body. The first chakra is called the root chakra and it is located at the base of the pubic bone.

Each chakra draws in different colored energy. The color of the energy that a chakra draws correlates with the colors of the rainbow. The root chakra draws in red energy. The next chakra above that, the second chakra, draws in orange energy and above that, yellow. After that is green, blue, purple, and finally violet at the top of the head.

The chakras are like fuel systems for the body and when they aren't working, the whole body, especially the area that chakra is in, may suffer health-wise. It is important that the chakras are functioning. I detect that a lot of the reason why the glandular system gets compromised is because the chakra supporting it is not functioning at full capacity.

For example, people with low thyroid use may do SFT taps to clear out blockages in their throat chakra.

(Say each statement three times while tapping on your head and say it a fourth time while tapping on your chest.)

"I remove all stagnant energy from my throat chakra; in all moments," and

"I recharge my throat chakra; in all moments."

Maybe someone has worked on clearing every one of their chakras and they still don't feel like they are working at ultimate capacity. Maybe their individual chakras are not working with the other chakras in the body. There may be some sort of disconnect somewhere. To remedy a disconnect between the chakras, the cranial tap would be:

"I align and connect all my chakras; in all moments."

Some people have done this and still have difficulty in clearing their chakras and feeding them clean energy. Some people have an aversion to working with the different colors of the chakra system. The reason is very subtle. Since the chakras are identified with different colors and to feed the chakras is to "ingest" different colors, one must have a good relationship with the colors involved.

For example, I had one client who had difficulty in clearing and reengineering her root chakra. It was creating a weakness in the body. I could tell that feeding the clean, red energy into the body wasn't helping when I detected the subtle cause. She had an aversion to the color red.

Because she had an aversion to the color red, she was inadvertently preventing red healing energy from entering her body. Because of this, her root chakra was depleted and she had sexual issues. It doesn't matter which came first and which is the cause of what. I realized then that if I helped her clear her repulsion to red (It could be as simple as hating to menstruate or as deep as a blood stained scenario after war), it would help in balancing out the energy of the body. Here are some taps for the root chakra color red:

"I release the belief that red is evil; in all moments."

"I release associating red with pain; in all moments."

"I release associating red with shame; in all moments."

One's association with a particular color may be very personal. They may have to realize what negative associations they may have to a particular color when they are clearing out their aversions.

Here are some taps to help with the clearing of the other chakras of the body:

"I release associating orange with hell; in all moments."

"I release associating green with putrid; in all moments."

"I release associating green with infection; in all moments."

"I release associating blue with sadness and tears; in all moments."

"I release associating purple with fear and shadows; in all moments."

You can make up whatever taps you need. Just think about every color and what it may conjure up for you. This just may be a back door means of clearing out your chakras, and by doing so, releasing stagnant energy from your system all by yourself.

5 CALIBRATE THE DAY

We choose the course of the day, week and even life with what we decide to "put out there" each moment. Did you already complain that it was Monday? Did you already have a negative thought about the weather? These things set precedent for the next moment.

Our mood is not set in stone. If we wake up a little bit irritated or with a scratchy throat, it may take a moment to forgo the disdain and calibrate the day to Joy. But this is a choice. Wake up your awareness by sitting still for a moment, breathing deep and paying attention to what your body is telling you. Address the needs so it doesn't vie for attention using negative thoughts and feelings.

Breakfast is a way to tune into your body and give it what it needs. Your daily routine of opening the curtains and letting the dog out are all ways to pour love into your moment. Every little task that is done consciously is pouring love into the day.

It is a beautiful fresh start to the new week. The days are getting longer. It will be warmer soon. How are you going to use your talents to uplift others? What thoughts are you going to add to the universal mind? What kindnesses are you going to express as a part of a universal heart? Love is here, encouraging you for your positive efforts.

(Say each statement three times while tapping on your head, and say it a fourth time while tapping on your chest.)

"I am a Powerhouse of Divine Light, Love, Song, Healing, Health, Joy, Beauty, Abundance and Wholeness; in all moments."

"Every cell of my body assimilates, resonates and emanates Divine Light, Love, Song, Healing, Health, Joy, Beauty, Abundance and Wholeness; in all moments."

"I am a conscious conduit for Divine Light, Love, Song, Healing, Health, Joy, Beauty, Abundance and Wholeness in the world; in all moments."

"All who broach me are invited to assimilate, resonate, and emanate with Divine Light, Love, Song, Healing, Health, Joy, Beauty, Abundance and Wholeness; in all moments."

"I perpetuate Divine Light, Love, Song, Healing, Health, Joy, Beauty, Abundance and Wholeness; in all moments."

6 DEALING WITH THESE "TRYING TIMES"

There has never been a time in history that was not a trying time. It is an aspect of life. The struggle for balance demands that we are always met with adversity. It is what hones us as Spiritual Beings.

If someone were in space and lived without gravity, their muscles would be so atrophied when they returned to earth that they wouldn't be able to lift their head off the ground. This puts into perspective how adversity strengthens us.

It takes an act of will to proceed in the face of the streams of negativity that bombard the average individual. We have to choose to be more than average. One way to empower ourselves is to strengthen the spirit by swimming upstream against the negative currents. An even better choice is to simply let them pass by. This exercises the spirit in a different way, by not engaging them.

Turn off the news. The human processing system was not designed to continually filter death and disaster around the globe.

Refuse to listen to gossip. Shut it down or walk away.

Forego challenging others' opinions and remove yourself from combative debates. It is an exercise in futility or an overindulgent ego.

Realize that truth is a subjective concept. Refuse to accept anyone's vantage point as completely yours.

Be grateful that others have an opposing view. It takes the pressure off to not have to be right all the time.

Don't judge others. You have abused power in the past. Allow others the same freedom to learn the consequences of their actions.

Every life is a compilation of miracles. The miracles that run the microcosm of your life are the same ones that perpetuate the macrocosm. Trust the process.

Live in gratitude as a means of flipping the switch from fear to Love.

Realize that man does not run the show. There are forces in the Universe that are in play far beyond the infancy of man's understanding.

Realize that every situation that arises always has a solution. It is part of the balance.

Realize that your thoughts and actions are part of the group consciousness. If you want a more positive world, think more positive thoughts and give little endorsement to the negative ones.

Recognize that truth has many vantage points. If you don't like your present point of truth, just change it.

All of these suggestions aren't easy to implement. Trying to use them is a means of strengthening spiritual muscles. It is much more empowering than being swept away in mass belief systems. True leaders challenge what the masses perceive as truth. By doing so in your corner of the world, you too become a great leader. It is inevitable.

7 HEALING THE CHAKRA SYSTEM

I had a private session with someone who was very structured. She relied on the structure of her day to keep herself grounded. When I tuned into her energy, I saw her root chakra was compromised. I saw it as beautiful energy spilling out of its containment through a "hole" in the side of it. It was very clear.

In the session, we repaired her root chakra. This is the tap that I gave her: (Say each statement three times while tapping on your head and say it a fourth time while tapping on your chest.)

"I repair and fortify the Wei Chi of my Root Chakra; in all moments."

If you get a sense that your chakras are compromised, you may want to do these other SFT taps as well. Compromised chakras would show up in different ways: feeling ungrounded, feeling spacey, feeling indecisive or ineffective, being too practical or fearful. Maybe these taps will help.

"I repair and fortify my Earth Star Chakra; in all moments."

"I repair and fortify my Root Chakra; in all moments."

"I repair and fortify my Sacral Chakra; in all moments."

"I repair and fortify my Solar Plexus Chakra; in all moments."

"I repair and fortify my Heart Chakra; in all moments."

"I repair and fortify my Throat Chakra; in all moments."

"I repair and fortify my Third Eye; in all moments."

"I repair and fortify my Crown Chakra; in all moments."

"I repair and fortify my Soul Star Chakra; in all moments."

"I align all my chakras; in all moments."

"I am centered in, and an extension of, Divine Love; in all moments."

8 DEVELOPING TAPS FOR OTHERS

I have always been very sensitive. I could perceive the slightest innuendo where others would see none. It was a difficult childhood. But every experience has been a building block for whom I have become.

I have always been a good listener, so intent on helping others. And when I went to massage therapy school, I learned to feel energy in someone's body. It got very easy to feel it for me. So easy, I didn't have to touch them to feel it. When I talked to people on the phone, I realized I not only could feel their energy but also unblock it with my intent to help.

Friends with severe issues would call me in the middle of the night to avoid the emergency room for things like diverticulosis or during the middle of a stroke. Their issues got addressed and symptoms never returned even though, at my insistence, they sought medical help. I have always wondered why people didn't have the abundance, relationship and health they so desired. It occurred to me that they set their own deprivation into motion by taking vows in past lifetimes of poverty, chastity, silence, etc. And there is where my work begins: helping them undo what they have set forth in the past and helping them realize that they are worthy in this lifetime, just forgetful of what they once put into motion.

SFT Tap to help:

(Say the statement three times while tapping on your head and say it a fourth time while tapping on your chest.)

"I recall all my missing parts; in all moments."

9 SELF-SABOTAGE

Many times we allow our concept of something to interfere with our enjoying the actuality of it. A perfect example of this is holidays. Many times we are so concerned with them looking like the image of what we think they should be that we shift out of enjoying what is at hand.

Here are some SFT taps or affirmations that may be helpful:

"I release allowing my concept of this holiday to interfere with the enjoyment of the day; in all moments."

"I release allowing my concept of abundance to interfere with enjoyment of living; in all moments."

"I release allowing my concept of marriage to interfere with my appreciation of my mate; in all moments."

"I release allowing my concept of God to interfere with the richness of my spiritual relationship with God; in all moments."

Develop your own. This is a good way to look at all the ways one may sabotage their own happiness.

A road can take you only as far as it goes. At some point, you are going to have to forge your own path.

10 FIGHTING OURSELVES

The way to honor Love, Truth, Innocence and Wisdom is to give, know, have and exude it.

A point of view becomes obsolete when it becomes acutely obvious of all those who are excluded from the benefits of that vantage point.

Scoff at the Dreamers and the "tree huggers," but they most likely have been the balance that has prevented the pragmatists from destroying us all thus far.

I draw from an infinite source of Love and Goodwill that I perpetually imbue to everyone everywhere.

It is easy to point out the obvious and shove negativity in another's face. But a person of Grace will ignore all the insults of life and perpetually sift for Gold and Light and Love.

I hold the intention of Joy, Love, Abundance, Freedom, Health, Success, Security, Companionship, Peace and Compassion for every being in the world.

Technique:

Instead of being annoyed with the crowds, imagine that everyone you interact with is an opportunity to show love to humanity. Smile, let others pass, be an example of kindness and teach others how to be a ripple of Love that is sent out in all directions.

11 WHEN FEELING SAD, ANGRY OR MOODY

Anything that stimulates the senses can cause angst. Foods, drinks, smells, visuals, sounds, people, places can all affect internal peace. Take inventory of what was happening the moment you felt angst and make efforts to remove it from your environment. This is your life and your responsibility to yourself to make it as wonderful and pleasant as possible.

Take a deep breath and visualize a beautiful bubble of Light in front of you. Visualize putting all the angst into the bubble and just sending it away.

12 YOU DESERVE WELLNESS

When one has an issue, many times they think the worst case scenario. Even when someone is deciding whether they are coming down with the flu or something, they have to ruminate over the signs before they validate themselves by telling others they are sick.

Then they feel the need to defend those issues. They don't want to sound ridiculous so they build up a case for being sick. They are, in a sense, coming into agreement with the illness. Then they identify with it by defending their need to nurture themselves by having it.

Being sick is a chance to opt out for a bit. It is an excuse to stay home, relinquish the diet, forgo the workload, spoil one's self, relax, take a break, focus on one's self, feel important, be the center of attention, ask for help, surrender to life, allow others to help and change priorities. Because people are used to invalidating themselves otherwise, being sick is their chance to get fulfillment, at first.

But then the novelty rubs off and the patient feels they have to return to "the grind" or up the ante on their illness. It is sad to think how many people up the ante. It is one of the main reasons dis-ease is so prevalent in society.

Here are some better ways: take a day off, go off the diet once in a while, spoil yourself, leave work at the office, be the center of attention, accept help, ask for help, change priorities, have fun, return to joy, return to ease. Create it! Demand it! Revel in it. What the human can endure is limited, but what the human spirit can tap into is infinite.

Here are some SFT taps to help:

(Say each statement three times while tapping on your head and say it a fourth time while tapping on your chest.)

"I release validating myself through illness; in all moments."

"I release using illness to relate to others; in all moments." (This may happen in genetic diseases.)

"I release my genetic propensity for disease; in all moments."

"I release carrying illness in my DNA; in all moments."

"I release using illness as a common ground; in all moments."

"I release being in agreement with illness; in all moments."

"I remove being cursed with illness; in all moments."

"I dissolve all karmic ties with illness; in all moments."

"I remove all the pain, burden and limitations that illness has put on me; in all moments."

"I take back all the Joy, Love, Abundance and Freedom that illness has taken from me; in all moments."

"I release resonating with illness; in all moments."

"I release all illness from my sound frequency; in all moments."

"I shift my paradigm from illness to Joy, Love, Abundance and Freedom; in all moments."

Let's return to Joy, Love, Abundance and Freedom. Those are birthrights worth striving for and what every loving parent wishes for their baby. You deserve a wonderful existence.

13 THE GOLDEN GLOBE HEART CHAKRA TECHNIQUE

We think of the heart chakra as one of a few energy systems in the body that funnels energy into the body. What if it were more? What if it were the gateway to our connection with infinite Love and Reverence? What if it were the key to our own divinity?

What if all our experiences of pain, torture and unworthiness were meant to deter this beautifully resilient component of ourselves? What if the mind were meant to distract from this truly empowering apparatus so that we could continue to exist in the illusionary worlds of matter? What if realizing the importance of the heart chakra was the key to our own omnipotence? What if gratitude, instead of a pleasant notion, was actually the breath of the heart chakra?

In the group session I facilitated, I was given an image and the importance of the heart chakra. I saw a standing globe of the world and how it spins freely in all directions. Then I felt the participants' backs open up and release all the lifetimes in which they had to protect their physical back. Then I saw them as human globe stands. They were here to be globes of love in which the heart chakra emanated love. The person that they are is merely here to hold a place for it.

The person that they are, with all their petty problems and concerns, was just the standing apparatus for the heart chakra. It held as much significance as a globe stand does for the accurate depiction of the world. We, in the human consciousness, make life all about the globe stand and forfeit the beautiful resonance of our divine purpose. Our divine purpose is to hold a place for the globe of love that is our heart chakra. We should allow ourselves to step out of the way and be all about the love.

In contemplation, see yourself deeply hollowed out at the chest. See a beautiful golden globe buoyed in that space and emanating light and love in every direction. It is not merely in the front. It is not leaning forward. It is symmetrical between the front and back. Feel how open your back is with your heart chakra being acknowledged there.

Feel how your whole beingness aligns and awakens with this truth. You are here to be love and to realize how to be more love. Everything else is merely holding a place for the love.

14 TRIGGERS

When figuring out what people are allergic to, doctors remove all potential causes from their diet and add items back into their diet one by one to see what the reaction is. This is a great technique to use in keeping your life balanced as well.

When starting this endeavor, it will be difficult to catch all of the contaminates for yourself. The key is getting to a point of emotional and mental balance so that you can take note of everything happening in your environment that brings dis-ease. A good time to start is the first thing in the morning.

When you wake up, pay attention to your mood. If it is a good one, it is a good time to start removing the triggers as they come. If it isn't a good one, you may want to look at the triggers from the night before. Sometimes foods and interactions the night before can cause a reaction, so these are things you can start dealing with from that awareness.

For example, if you have eaten a certain food the night before or watched a scary movie and had a nightmare, you may know enough to avoid those so as not to have the same effect. Use this technique to comb through everything that is causing the slightest discomfort. It will get to the point where you can control every situation and environmental cause that seemed impossible a short time before. At least you may know what is pulling you out of balance.

When you wake up in a peaceful state, it is easy to stay mindful of NOT feeling peaceful. At the first sign that your mood is changing, make a note of what is transpiring. That is a means of figuring out the once unconscious triggers. And some of them are subtle. It can be something as innocuous as wearing polyester (believe it or not this is a BIG one), or an outfit that you wore when you were in a bad mood and didn't wash yet. That is how subtle some triggers can be.

Other triggers are: certain people, music, watching television or certain shows, certain scents, activities that trigger unpleasant events, problems not dealt with, etc. Triggers are basically anything you think, feel, say, do, anyone you interact with or don't interact with, anything that engages any of the five senses or even the lack of stimulant. The more you are mindful of and able to eliminate the unconscious triggers, the more conscious you can live. It will also help you get a better handle on the triggers that you thought you could NOT control, like other people, their circumstances and even dis-ease.

15 IF YOU ARE AFRAID OF A CERTAIN EXPERIENCE

If you are afraid of a certain experience, realize that you are afraid of it because of something unpleasant that happened in your past in relationship to it.

You already have had a bad experience with the thing that you fear so you don't need that experience again. By consciously realizing that one issue, you can actually shift yourself into expecting a positive outcome when facing the thing that you fear.

16 AN ENERGETIC REASON FOR CHRONIC PAIN

The energetic reason for some injuries is because of our wanting to NOT have to use power to defend ourselves. In many past lives, we needed to hold a weapon in one hand and a shield in another. It was habit. We were in so many battles that it got tiring and made us weary. On some level, we now say to ourselves, "Never again! I would rather cut off my right arm than hurt another person with power plays." Many times in this day and age, the power plays are not physical, but they still trigger the same old issue. As an old Soul, it is much easier to be in pain than to watch someone else suffer.

Sometimes we are put in the position of having to protect ourselves. When this happens, our conviction of not hurting another being redirects the energy flow in a particular body part to "back up on us" and causes misalignment of our energy. We jam our energy up so as not to hurt another being. Sword in one hand, shield in another hand! We are so tired of it, we pull that energy back and suffer with the consequences. In many of my clients with carpal tunnel syndrome, I have seen what I'm describing as an underlying cause.

But with awareness, one can realize what they are subconsciously doing and reverse the process. It is possible to redirect one's energy flow with visualizations. Imagine a strong current of pure light coming down through the top of the head into the body and flowing completely through it. Visualize energy going through each limb and flushing out any debris. Imagine seeing energy flow out each finger and toe. See yourself simply as a tube with Divine Light running through it.

Bones and tissue are more pliable than we tend to believe. When the heart, mind and soul want to really change something, things we call miracles can happen.

17 HOMESICKNESS

During a session once, I was tuning into a client and she seemed to have two parallel energy cores running through her body. We all have energy flowing into us that is received through the Crown Chakra (soft spot on a baby's head) and flows through all the Chakras and aligns us with the energy of the Universe. I experience it as a column of energy. This client had two conflicting lines right next to each other. Each was trying to be dominant.

The energy conflict was a manifestation of one of the big issues on her agenda. She was afraid of losing her home. The home is the outer source of recharging one's energy. It is a form of comfort. But the true sanctuary of a person is in an existence that doesn't rely on the outer home. This person has a rich spiritual life but she also relies heavily on her outer home for spiritual sustenance. This conflict was creating an inner split in her energy core and weakening her.

When we put all our stock in the outward home, we can be devastated if our outer sanctuary is destroyed. To prevent this from happening, we must always stay aligned with our core. This is what the people who are devastated by losing everything are fortunate to learn from the experience.

Technique to use when you are homesick:

To strengthen your core, imagine what it would be like to lose everything. This is not to put anything into motion but to examine where your attachments are. Use time in your contemplations to release the strong reactions to the items that you are most vested in. To do this, visualize your dearest items converted into Love and with your imagination absorb the Love into yourself. If it is the home itself, convert the home into Love and siphon it all into you. In using this technique, you will get more grounded with the realization that you are never without the Love.

18 EMBEDDED SOULS

I facilitated a session with a woman who was going to her hometown. The initial sense was to release all her connection with it and all the karmic pulls it had on her which we did. But the session took on a more profound aspect.

In the session, I saw the earth. Just as blood seeps into the ground, I saw people dying in layer upon layer into the ground and being embedded there. There wasn't always the convenience of honoring each body as it fell. And souls didn't always conveniently walk into the light. In the history of earth, due to war, indifference or inability, the dead lay where they fell and sometimes their energy just dripped into the ground. That is what I saw.

It seemed that some of my client's energies were still entangled with the ground where she had fallen in a past life. It was time to collect herself. And to make the most of the session, we used her as a surrogate to collect the energies of all others who have fallen and assist them as well. Why do this? Because I was directed to and given the insight to release them.

In a vision that was happening simultaneously as I facilitated her session, I saw the client and myself on the side of a dark hill seeped and layered with energies. Behind us stood our spirit guides. This woman is very attuned to her purpose, so she was open to assist in this. What I saw was her and me with our arms outstretched pulling up energies from the ground. They were in the form of people. We pulled them up from the ground and sent them back to where they originated.

At first, we did this for her hometown. Then I envisioned the earth and we did the same thing globally. After her session, she was to get on her flight and fly home. She reported that she never has experienced such a peaceful and restful flight.

19 ALLEVIATING DIS-EASE

When a friend is fighting a life changing illness, here are some of the things I suggest to them. They realize that I am not a medical doctor and all suggestions are meant to enhance their medical professional's assistance.

- Remove all scented items from the environment: Perfume, candles, other scented personal items. They are all chemicals that add stress to the body.

- Stop using antiperspirants. Switch to a deodorant. Sweat is a means to release toxins. To prevent the sweating is to prevent the release of the poisons.

- Wear only natural fibers. Wearing synthetic fibers is like wearing a plastic tarp. It cuts off the breathing process of the skin.

- Remove all toxic people and situations from your environment. Physical dis-ease is a result of emotional issues that have become so entrenched in the energetic body that they bleed through to affect the physical body as well.

- Take osage orange tincture. It is known to starve cancer cells.

- Stop eating dairy. Many older people are concerned with bone density so they over compensate by loading up on dairy. This is not helpful.

- Kill the parasites in your body. Parasite cleanses can be tedious and difficult. The easier way to kill the parasites is to get a TENS unit and run a low electric current through the body. This will kill the parasites and is more effective than the walnut tincture and wormwood because it is not deterred by the blood brain barrier and can cleanse the brain of parasites too.

- Don't tell people about your health issues. Everyone has their opinions about illness. Their thoughts, emotions and experiences can have a negative affect on your situation.

- Take time to center each day. Visualize infinite Light and Love coming into the top of your head and saturating your whole body and dissolving everything that is not Love and Light.

- Send yourself Love. The cells of your body have a consciousness and, as such, they want to be appreciated.

- Get plenty of hugs and love from a good pet.

- Say only kind things about yourself. Monitor your thoughts and only speak and think uplifting ones. Be consciously grateful.

- Don't own a diagnosis. It is not yours. If something is yours, you are going to get attached to it and have more trouble getting rid of it. Think of it more as an experience that is passing through.

These are just a very few things to help one's self. They are a good practice for all.

20 A CURSE

A curse is simply derailing someone from their current course of action by superimposing it with your intention fueled by passion, self righteousness or malice. Feel how doing this simple exercise lifts a heaviness from you. Because when you sabotage someone else, either intentionally or on purpose, it affects your own well being.

(Say each statement three times while tapping on your head and say it a fourth time while tapping on your chest.)

"I remove all curses that I have ever put on anyone or anything; in all moments."

21 THE ENERGETIC SIGNIFICANCE OF THE "HEIL HILTER" SALUTE

People who are onlookers wonder why the people of Germany did not revolt against Hitler. How could they stand by and allow him to reign with such unquestioned authority? A big part of it had to do with the energetic mechanism of the "Heil Hitler" salute.

Hitler studied esoteric practices. He infused his reign with practices that were allowing him to psychically control the masses. He used the symbol of Thor's Hammer to depict his regime. Many know it better as the swastika now. What he did was take the energetic significance of this dynamic symbol that was already infused with power and harness it to his cause. Then he claimed ownership of it.

That is the same intention the group ISIL had in using the name of a female Goddess as their name. Their intention was to desecrate Goddess energy by harnessing the empowerment of the word to their will. That is why it is very good NOT to call that group ISIS. By calling them by the name of Goddess, you are conceding to them taking from female energy everywhere and allowing them to use its essence to reign in terror.

When our government REFUSES to label this group as terrorists and refuses to name them, they are actually doing so because they understand, on some level, spiritual law. When you name something, you agree to it. You make space for it in your culture. You solidify its existence. Not labeling it is a way to not open the door to it. This is a very savvy spiritual practice.

There are dirty rich billionaires that are running commercials that demonize our government for not labeling the terrorists' crimes and defining them better. These possibly could be the same filthy rich billionaires that make money off of war by selling guns and ammunition to both sides. They understand spiritual law as well and use it to hoard wealth. They prey on people's ignorance and fear to keep them pliable to giving up their energy. It is a sick game of chess for them where they run both sides of the board. The more that people understand the dynamics of energy, the more this sick game can be ruined for them.

When Hitler had people hold up their hand in a forceful salute directed at him, he was "shaking the crowd down" for their energy. Energy runs freely through our body and comes out forcibly through the palms of the hand at will. Everyone is an energy system and everyone has this mechanism, whether they understand it or not.

When people were holding up their palms to Hitler, they were sending all their energy to him to use as his source of power. That is why he was unstoppable. The people were feeding him their energy. It is no different than having every crowd empty all their pockets and give all their cash over to him to run his political reign. This is what was demanded of them every time they gathered. They were kept in a state of depletion and compliance this way. When they were made to salute any Nazi leader, the leader would then turn it over to their higher ups until it funneled back to Hitler. This was a very efficient system of depleting the people.

When the raising of the palms is done in church, it is the same principle. People are giving their energy to the church. They agree to this and trust that it is going to God, but it is not. It is going to the running of the church. At this point in evolution, if God was sentient, there would be a wish that all people hang on to their energy and understand how to live empowered. That is what my writings help people understand how to do. God does not want you to give away your power. God wants you to remain empowered but share fluidly in love.

As far as Trump is concerned, he knows what he is doing when he has people pledge to him. He knows they are feeding him their energy. He is playing with power right now. He knows that the pledge is a form of people giving up their energy to him. He is testing the limits of how it feels to be a demigod. He's enjoying his power trip.

What he doesn't realize is that there is a person in the viewing audience who is very savvy to the ways of energy. I am not going to allow him to prey on people's ignorance to fleece them of their energy. No one should be willing to hand over their energy in such a way anymore. Because they have been so conditioned, they do this.

I have interrupted him from taking from others energetically. This would sound crazy if someone else said it, but those who have worked with me in private and group sessions know I have this capability. I have done at least that for them to get them their empowerment back. I am using my gifts to prevent mass enslavement by a power monger.

No, the world is not about mass slavery anymore. As much as people are fighting to stay in their cages, there are great souls coaxing them out of them. It is tedious to stay perched with the cage door open and wait for the nipping scared dog of humanity to stop biting me and allow me to help them out of their prison. Perhaps I am gaining their trust. Perhaps they will get an innate sense of maintaining their sense of self.

Until then, I will be saving humans from themselves. Trump may think that he wants to be adored and is enjoying the euphoria of his ride. But people must not be allowed, in their amusement of him, to allow their will to be worn down to his agenda.

So as a technique, every time that one sees or hears the word Trump, they can imagine taking the concept of him that the media is growing and breaking it apart like a clump of clay. Break apart the word Trump and see all the energy that was building up that clump scurry back to its original owner. You can do this with any group that collects the energy of others and uses it for its own agenda.

22 SHATTER ALL ILLUSION

In contemplation, visualize yourself in a huge glass maze. You are walking through this maze looking for truth and love. The maze itself is immersed in truth and love, but you cannot see it because of the vantage point of being in the maze.

On the walls of the maze are all these images that make you identify with you. They have your home life, work and all that is comfortable. Unfortunately, they also have all the things that cause fear and unhappiness as well. On one side of each corridor is the concept that you are striving for to have more love. On the opposite corridor, is the thing that represents something of love and truth to you but falls short of the absolute love and truth outside the maze.

From a vantage point of standing outside the maze, throw heavy rocks at the maze and shatter all the walls of it so that the illusion is destroyed. Continue doing this until the you that was in the maze is standing free and clear of any walls of illusion. Imagine walking around crushing the shattered glass into a fine powder by stepping on it.

Feel yourself expansive in the clear surroundings of truth and love. All illusion is gone.

(Say each statement three times while tapping on your head and say it a fourth time while tapping on your chest.)

"I declare myself a surrogate for all life in doing these taps; in all moments."

"I shatter the illusion of religion; in all moments."

"I shatter the illusion of God; in all moments."

"I shatter male domination; in all moments."

"I shatter the illusion of female inferiority; in all moments."

"I shatter all power-plays; in all moments."

"I shatter all universal lies; in all moments."

"I shatter all universal manipulation; in all moments."

"I shatter all illusion of the benefits of war; in all moments."

"I shatter all war; in all moments."

"I shatter all universal ego; in all moments."

"I shatter all egos; in all moments."

"I shatter all illusion of dis-ease; in all moments."

"I shatter all illusion of beauty; in all moments."

"I shatter all illusion of perfection; in all moments."

"I shatter all ugliness; in all moments."

"I shatter all flaws; in all moments."

"I shatter all illusion of aging; in all moments."

"I shatter all illusion of youth; in all moments."

"I shatter all aging; in all moments."

"I shatter all illusion of death; in all moments."

"I shatter all illusion of separation; in all moments."

"I shatter all want; in all moments."

"I shatter all need; in all moments."

"I shatter all judgment; in all moments."

"I shatter all illusion of lack; in all moments."

"I shatter all slavery; in all moments."

"I shatter all illusion of freedom; in all moments."

"I shatter all indifference; in all moments."

"I shatter all apathy; in all moments."

"I shatter all darkness; in all moments."

"I shatter all illusion of wealth; in all moments."

"I shatter all poverty; in all moments."

"I shatter all ignorance; in all moments."

"I shatter all power; in all moments."

"I shatter all fear; in all moments."

"I shatter all unworthiness; in all moments."

"I shatter all illusion of humility; in all moments."

"I shatter all illusion of love; in all moments."

"I shatter all debauchery; in all moments."

"I shatter all evil; in all moments."

"I am centered and empowered in absolute loving truth; in all moments."

"I resonate, emanate, and am interconnected with all life in absolute love and truth; in all moments."

23 TECHNIQUE FOR HEART DISEASE AND HIGH BLOOD PRESSURE

When you can "hear" your blood pressure or feel your heart pumping fast, take a deep breath and sink into yourself. Take another breath and sink some more. With each breath, feel yourself sink as much as possible. When you have sunk as much as possible, visualize your energy spreading out. You may notice that the energy in your heart is thick. Visualize sticking a straw into it and siphoning out the thick gunky energy. Siphon it into a bubble of light and send it away. See it dissolve into the light.

Then put all your attention on your heart. See it in a deflated sack. Visualize blowing Love into the sack until your heart is saturated in Light and is free-standing in a clear strong globe of Light. Hear the Bee Gees' song "Staying Alive" playing in the background and calm the heart down so it is beating in rhythm with the song. If you want to be silly (humor is relaxing), see your heart dancing on a disco dance floor with a strobe light. See the whole heart sack (pericardium) filled up with incredible Light.

Visualize the purity and the magnitude of that Light flowing through the valves leading out of the heart and into the body. Visualize it being so strong and pure that it dissolves all the stagnant energy that is in the arteries until they are all clear passages. See the purity continue all the way to the veins and clean out the veins as well. Sense the energy loop around the body in a fluid, cohesive, calm rhythm. Feel the Love literally coursing through your veins.

Visualize changing your vantage point so that you see your body as the globe of Light with the loops of Lights coming and going from it and seeing it as a pure flowing structure. Practice doing this technique many times until you can conjure it up in moments and give good energy to your heart and whole cardiovascular system at will.

24 ANTACID HEALING TECHNIQUE

See all the atoms in your body and see them all working together. But if any aren't, plop in a couple of antacid tablets. They are cells that are happy, effervescent, exponentially overflowing with joy and enthusiasm. See them contagious to the whole. When you plop them in the body of atoms, see the whole body come alive effervescently with swirling, expansive, interactive energy. See the whole body become as enlivened as a Van Gogh sky. See the body come more enlivened and interactive in swirls of color, light and even beautiful music with the whole world. Observe until the whole world is joyful and brimming with spontaneous swirling, healing energy that encompasses and saturates all the atoms of you as well.

25 CURSING

If people are having a hard life and don't understand why, but are still cursing, they are disconnected from cause and effect. Why do you think it is called cursing? Because people who curse are spitting out curses left and right. They are cursing life, the world, others, themselves and everyone and everything in their path.

It is so ridiculous to expect life to hand you out gifts and kindness if you go around cursing it. If you curse regularly, then you are not the victim of life. You are the abuser.

If people really want a better life, then they will take the responsibility to not curse anymore. They will abstain from this one very selfish indulgence and will see how the world around them responds. When people swear when communicating with me, they are sending out an energetic blow dart of anger. It is rude, indulgent and unnecessary.

26 HOW TO RID YOUR FACE OF WRINKLES

If you can get this simple concept, you can get rid of all the laugh lines and wrinkles on your face. Have you ever had a comforter or pillow that got all bunched up and needed to be fluffed? All the insides may have collected in one corner of the pillow or comforter and you are left with a lot of extra material with no filling? That is all wrinkles are. That is it!

The fluffy "meat" of your face has collected and kind of solidified into the cartilage and sinewy material on top of the facial bone. But it can be undone. What you do is press firmly, but carefully, through the lines on your face to the cartilage beneath. Work on one spot first to get the hang of it. The crows feet is the easiest way to see evidence of your intention.

Press through the crows feet to the surface below. If you find a tender bump, hold firm pressure on it for however long it takes for it to dissolve. At first, as you press, it will seem to get firmer and harder. But then as you hold it, it will melt into your body. This is you releasing trapped energy within your face. Once you feel this, you will be encouraged to do it more.

Venture around your facial bones to all the places where the skin is not taut. Get the hang of manipulating the cartilage to make it more pliable. If you have a heavy lid, work along the brow bone underneath the eyebrow. Notice how your skin feels uncomfortable but excitingly tight afterwards. When you are watching TV, make this a daily routine. You will be surprised at how easily the wrinkles disappear.

It is good to stay hydrated of course, but this technique works more deeply and proactively than merely staying hydrated.

27 COPING WITH STRESS AND EATING DISORDERS

Eating is one of the most primal urges. There may be a disconnect between the desire for food in this lifetime and the deprivation of past lifetimes. We forget how vital food is for survival. Even though it seems like a less important need, food for the body is as elemental as the body's need for oxygen.

Compulsive overeaters have experienced starvation in past lifetimes. When they are in binge mode, their brain is in primal mode. The desire to eat overrides mental rationality. The same survival mode also overrides the body signals of being full.

A technique to use when someone is a binge eater is to visualize being in the lifetime that they starved in. Imagine feeding THAT body as opposed to the present body. That is why binge eaters never get full; they are not present when they are eating so they never register as full. It's also why the dieting technique of conscious eating is effective. When we're consciously eating, we're bringing our emotional self into the present.

Some of us are so stuck in starvation mode that it's nearly impossible to be present when we eat. We are emotionally trapped in a past experience. The key to overriding this is to consciously bring the food we are presently eating into the other experience. This brings the food we are eating and the hunger we're feeling into alignment. When we aren't consciously eating, it is like bringing food up to your mouth but never having it connect. Bringing the food of the present into the starvation of the past is an empowering technique of feeding the desire behind the food.

Another technique to satisfy a compulsive desire for food is the cotton candy technique. Since the sun is an important energy supply, visualize the sun as a huge burst of edible energy in the form of cotton candy. During the day, visualize pulling off tufts of sun energy and eating it through the day. Feel it dissolve in your mouth, satiate and energize you. Since action follows thought, you will actually be supplying a deep form of comfort to your body.

Many people vacillate between feeling insecure and sensing the awesome omnipotence of their true self. This creates a skewed self-image. Someone can feel really great about themselves and then look in the mirror and feel huge. They actually perceive their own energy field. It is much larger than their physical body. If people could separate their energy field from their physical body, they wouldn't feel so confused when they look in the mirror and see a big presence. They would accept the illusion of what they see in the mirror and realize that it is good to have a huge presence. It is ridiculous to try and starve an energy field. There is a way to draw in your energy field but it has nothing to do with food deprivation.

When someone throws up constantly, they are really stressed personalities. Food represents energy to them. Since they have excess energy in the form of stress, they throw up as a way to literally release the stress. There are many techniques to release the stress, but it has nothing to do with food deprivation.

The easiest way to alleviate stress are techniques that were developed by a man named Lester Levinson. They have developed into two disciplines. One is called the Sedona Method and the other is called the Release Technique. Lester Levinson discovered that stress has a weight and a mass. If there were the right intricate machinery, your stress could actually be measured.

Levinson taught that stress is trapped energy. It wants to be released. If you want to get rid of stress, just visualize opening up your stomach and your chest and visualize the stress being sucked out by a Universal Vacuum Cleaner. It would look similar to how the air would come rushing out of an opened door on an airplane. Try this technique and see if it helps alleviate stress.

Another technique that is based on the teachings of Lester Levinson is a twist on the vacuum technique. When you are feeling stress being drawn into your lower stomach, it is uncomfortable because it's being stored there until your body can process it. Instead of drawing the stress in, visualize a muscle in the lower stomach blowing the energy out. Develop this sensation and using it can be as simple as changing a setting on your vacuum cleaner.

Once you have figured how to do this, think of things that have caused a stress reaction in your body. At the same time, switch the setting on the stomach to blow the energy out. If you experience a big yawn and a sense of being lighter, you have successfully released your own stress. I believe eating disorders are more about stress and feeling ineffective than about food. The techniques I have suggested are meant to empower.

Both techniques are proven ways for healers to stay balanced. I also suggest that you share this message with anyone you know who is stressed or has an eating disorder.

28 GROWING OLD

When one is afraid of growing old, it is clear that they have already made an agreement with it. They may hear all the time, "Don't ever get old." But that just instills in them that there is something to fear. The real fear is watching others' agreement with aging and mimicking it. What is worse is partaking in a group consensus on it.

When we watch others do anything, we learn from them. We identify closely with our parents and believe that what they have experienced will be our experience. I recently had a client who had real foggy thoughts. Her mother had dementia so she was afraid she was developing it. In the images I saw of her mother, she was cooking big pots of tomato sauce out of aluminum pots. The dementia was exacerbated, if not caused by, the aluminum in her cooking pots. The daughter did not have to worry about this as she did. She did not have to use symptoms of a dis-ease to hold her mother close.

There is such an habitual component to aging. It does not have to be accepted as inevitable. I know this will annoy many who are experiencing what they call, "the decline." But forgoing the mindset of aging can reduce a lot of inconvenience that longevity may otherwise bring.

Here are some SFT taps to assist in the matter of longevity:

(Say each statement three times while tapping on your head and say it a fourth time while tapping on your chest.)

"I recant all vows and agreements between myself and aging; in all moments."

"I release associating longevity with debilitation; in all moments."

"I release the fear of longevity; in all moments."

"I remove all curses between myself and aging; in all moments."

"I release the belief that debilitation is inevitable with longevity; in all moments."

"I release mimicking genetic traits of debilitation that are in my family; in all moments."

"I release expecting debilitation; in all moments."

"I shift my paradigm to seeing aging as a wonderful adventure; in all moments."

29 REVERSE THE AGING PROCESS: TECHNIQUE TO REJUVENATE YOUR ENDOCRINE SYSTEM

In contemplation, pinpoint a certain time in a younger version of you when you can remember being present, aware, grateful and productive. Look at that version of you and get a sense of remembering what it was like to be that you. In a very focused way, overlay that version of you onto you in the present. Overlay it on you and be totally focused on that version of you and allow it to sink into you.

Careful. DO NOT DO THIS IN THE OPPOSITE. Do not overlay yourself on top of the younger version of you. There may be a natural tendency to do that. But do not visit the present you into the past for this particular technique. Bring that version of you into the present.

When you have the younger version of you overlaid on top of you, visualize securing it to you in some way. Either clip it around the edges or glue it on top or just hold it in place. See it bulky on top of you, but hold tight to the younger version of you. You can even perceive the present you moving around underneath trying to break through. Allow the younger you to prevail.

Hold the younger version over the present version of you until there is no more struggle. Hold down until all the thicknesses are smoothed out and all the lumps are gone. Allow the present you to disintegrate. Be only aware of the younger you in its place.

Shift your attention back into the present and look out of your body through the new set of younger eyes. Feel a sense of youth and empowerment. Forgo talking or focusing on anything that the old you would have focused or talked about. Retrain your dialogue to match the younger you.

30 HEALING THROUGH SELF-AWARENESS

We are all creating and affecting everything around us at such a deep level. Our attitude and thoughts are somehow little beacons that are either encouraging or wilting everything in our Universe.

I had an experience with a client. He had a numb area in his leg. As I worked on it in his session, he fell asleep. When he awoke, he described what he experienced. He saw little faces in square windows. Most of them were asleep. But when he was looking at them, they started to wake up, and one of them perked up and looked right back at him.

He said they were the cells in his leg. He was brought to tears at the sweetness of the little faces and how they perked up from his attention. He displayed a love for the faces that was very sacred to observe. In that moment, he was actually waking up to loving himself by loving the individual cells of his own body. He was experiencing his own consciousness. It was a moment that has helped me in how I assist others.

I thought of all the ramifications. How often do we yell at our children and loved ones? How often do we say negative things to them and to ourselves? Are we making them sick? Are we making ourselves sick? Are there faces in all our cells looking up at us for love and attention? How easy would it be to give it to them? Are they all coexisting or are they being sent different messages?

I believe this technique is a powerful form of self-healing: Visualize all the cells in your body as a metropolis. The cells of the nerves and veins could be the transit system. The brain and heart could be different city centers, etc. See the cells of each area as the little faces looking out of little windows. See them awake, attentive and happy. If you get a sense that any of them in any area are asleep, then lovingly wake them up. And if you have a dis-ease in a particular part of the body, spend extra time nurturing those little faces.

Also, when you are trying to lose weight, just give extra love to the muscle cells. You don't need to berate yourself anymore. Just put all the attention on loving the muscle cells while totally ignoring the fat cells. It may help you feel proactive on a cellular level without the need to berate yourself. I hope this fun technique helps you as much as it helps me.

31 ENERGETIC LIPOSUCTION

To streamline a certain part of the body, a straw like instrument will be inserted into the area to suck out the fat. The fat is a carrying case for an emotional issue. If you have trouble losing weight, perhaps it is the emotional issues that you need to release. Perhaps if you release the emotional issue, the fat will have no purpose and will leave as well.

Visualize inserting a liposuction tube into your body and sucking out the emotional issue that is being carried by a fat cell. Imagine sucking out all the issues and trauma out of your body through this tube and imagine it being sent into a processing system where it is recycled back into pure love. All things return to love at one point.

See if you feel lighter and more free.

Use this issue if you are having pain in anyone area or discomfort of any kind. There are many different uses for this technique that you may discover on your own. But think of more subtle issues like shyness or sexual inhibition being addressed using this technique.

32 TECHNIQUE FOR CELLULAR HEALING

You know those pastry bags that are used to pipe cream into pastry? In contemplation, visualize filling one of those with clear, luscious, luminescent love. Visualize it as the most pure love that you could possibly acquire. Go to a part of your body that has been dealing with a lot of issues and pipe this incredible love into every cell of that area one by one. Visualize your cells like little pastries puffs and fill each one of them with incredible love.

If anything oozes out, let it. See it as the stagnant energy that has been causing dis-ease. Let it spill all over the place and then just visualize getting a wet-vac out and vacuuming up all the stagnant energy.

33 TAPS TO CONCEIVE A HEALTHY BABY

You will forget after you get pregnant that these taps helped you so...

YOU ARE WELCOME!

(Say each statement three times while tapping on your head, and say it a fourth time while tapping on your chest.)

"I flush my uterus clean; in all moments."

"I remove all emotional issues in regards to conceiving; in all moments."

"I remove all issues hindering the conception of my baby; in all moments."

"I remove all stress from the process of conceiving; in all moments."

"I remove all blockages from my fallopian tubes; in all moments."

"I flush clean my kidneys; in all moments."

"I flush clean my liver; in all moments."

"I flush clean my heart; in all moments."

"I flush clean our DNA; in all moments."

"I flush clean our chromosomes; in all moments."

"I remove all desperation to conceive; in all moments."

"I remove the fear of not conceiving; in all moments."

"I remove all selfish motives in regards to conceiving; in all moments."

"I extract all need and want from the process of conceiving; in all moments."

"I release all unworthiness in regards to conceiving; in all moments."

"I empower the sperm; in all moments."

"I empower the egg; in all moments."

"I make space in my womb for the sperm to fertilize the egg; in all moments."

"I remove all blockages to the sperm fertilizing the egg; in all moments."

"I stretch the capacity for the sperm to fertilize the egg; in all moments."

"I make space in my womb for the egg to accept the sperm; in all moments."

"I remove all blockages to the egg accepting the sperm; in all moments."

"I stretch the egg's capacity to accept the sperm; in all moments."

"The sperm is centered and empowered in fertilizing the egg; in all moments."

"The egg is centered and empowered in accepting the sperm; in all moments."

"I make space in this world to conceive, gestate and give birth to a healthy baby; in all moments."

"I remove all blockages to conceiving, gestating and giving birth to a healthy baby; in all moments."

"I stretch my capacity to conceive, gestate and give birth to a healthy baby; in all moments."

"I am centered and empowered in conceiving, gestating and giving birth to a healthy baby; in all moments."

"I resonate, emanate in confidence in conceiving, gestating and giving birth to a healthy baby; in all moments."

34 PEOPLE WILL SPEAK OF PROBLEMS AND ILLNESSES

People will speak of problems and illnesses as if they are things they are proud to own. They will say things like "my headache," "my bad credit," etc. If you claim to own something, it is harder to distance yourself from it.

Technique:

Pay attention to the things you are owning. When is the last time you heard someone say, "my Joy" or "my great health?" Only own things that you really value to have in your life. The word "My" is glue that paints issues into your energy field with long even strokes.

35 PROCEDURES

When a diagnosis is given, the person is usually blindsided. Then come the procedures. Procedures are intrusions to the body. All through history, cutting and probing the body was not a good thing. It meant death or torture. That is how the subconscious is wired to consider such invasions.

It is very important to talk to your own body and let it know what is happening. Make sure that you explain to it that you are not allowing it to be hurt, but are trying to help it. Pamper yourself, and give yourself extra love to help your body respond better for you.

One would think the body would know everything because it is present during the doctor's visits. But the body does not think. That is the mind. If one is not totally connected via body and mind then the body is left in the dark and may get its information through the thoughts and emotions.

If one can think their thoughts positive and their emotions uplifting, then the body will be more resilient.

36 REMOVING TOXIC ANGER

Anger is a toxic, corrosive poison that seeps into our lives in many ways. It is a byproduct of generations of invalidation and mistreatment and seeps into us directly or indirectly from others. It is as if the modern environment has showerheads of anger shooting out in all directions and we are its collecting rods and human holding tanks.

How can we deal with it? There are ways to get rid of it. Recycling it into productive energy like work, service or exercise seems to be effective. But all too often, instead of being dissipated, it is passed on to those around us. Or we keep pooling it within ourselves, accepting more and more from those around us and creating more space for it until we become totally explosive or withdraw into passivity.

Prayer or meditation can help you rise above the level of anger, but it doesn't dissipate the bubbling pool that already exists.

Here is a technique to dissipate the anger:

In contemplation, instead of avoiding the anger, go to it. Visualize a bubbling toxic pool of noxious energy within you. See it in its pure form. Look at how it has killed all life around it. Sense the hopelessness of allowing this pool to exist. Visualize calling upon a special, unique group of hazmat angels that are specifically equipped to deal with the toxic waste of anger.

Visualize them installing a pump and siphoning all the toxic anger out of the pool. See it going into a special pipe that dumps it into a river of light. Watch the waste flow into the Light and transform into a light golden energy as well.

Watch the hazmat angels work diligently to dry up the pool within you. See the scorched, burned, barren ground underneath it. But see it as totally bone dry. Watch as the angels install a drainage system where the pool once was and have it connect through a pipe directly into the river of Light.

Now see them use a hose to spray the ground and surrounding areas with a special treatment of healing energies. Watch a new growth of green grass emerge, then little flowers. Visualize them continuing to spray until a whole garden is formed. See the butterflies return. Hear birds singing. Visualize the sun coming out and see the scene lighter; watch as a rainbow emerges.

Remember how it felt to get rid of this pool. If you ever feel angry, call upon the hazmat angels to check the drain pipe and to remove blockages that may be plugging it up and creating a backwash of anger. When a situation arises that creates anger, be excited to use it as an opportunity to get rid of the anger by using this technique.

Share this technique with others instead of allowing them to use you as a drainage ditch for their anger.

37 HEAL YOUR HEART

(Say each statement three times while tapping on the top of your head and say it a fourth time while tapping on your chest.)

"I release pouring pain, frustration and helplessness into my heart; in all moments."

"I remove all the pain, frustration and helplessness from my heart; in all moments."

"I pour Joy, Love, Gratitude and Resiliency into my heart; in all moments."

"I repair and fortify the integrity, resiliency and function of my heart; in all moments."

"I am centered and empowered in a joyful, loving, abundant, healthy and resilient heart; in all moments."

"I release pouring pain, frustration and helplessness into my back; in all moments."

"I remove all the pain, frustration and helplessness from my back; in all moments."

"I pour Joy, Love, Gratitude and Resiliency into my back; in all moments."

"I repair and fortify the integrity, resiliency and function of my back; in all moments."

"I am centered and empowered in a joyful, loving, abundant, healthy and resilient back; in all moments."

"I release pouring pain, frustration and helplessness into my nervous system; in all moments."

"I remove all the pain, frustration and helplessness from my nervous system; in all moments."

"I pour Joy, Love, Gratitude and Resiliency into my nervous system; in all moments."

"I repair and fortify the integrity, resiliency and function of my nervous system; in all moments."

"I am centered and empowered in a joyful, loving, abundant, healthy and resilient nervous system; in all moments."

38 SINUS ISSUES

I facilitated a session once with someone who had severe sinus issues. During their session, we discovered part of the reason for the sinus trouble. I was given the image of them getting blindsided in a past life with a huge club. Their skull had been crushed. I had them do this tap:

"I release the trauma of having my skull bashed in; in all moments."

The information that accompanied the memory was that the sinus cavities being full was a protection for the body. When the sinus cavities were hollow, the head was feeling more vulnerable to being cracked open in this life. The only way the body could feel safe from this past trauma was to fill up those cavities with fluid.

It is often this way with our issues. We curse or complain about our body when the thing it is doing is a form of compensating for past trauma. It is defending itself. We show our ignorance and lack of loyalty to ourselves when we show little appreciation or respect for its service to us.

39 THE UNDERSTANDING OF PHYSICAL PAIN

I always get frustrated when there are campaigns to find cures for particular diseases. It's very frustrating because common sense dictates that the rise in dis-ease of the body would directly relate to the amount of toxins that the body is ingesting. Anything that is experienced by the senses needs to be processed by the body.

With my hands on work, I have experienced how emotional toxins cause physical pain. Doctors call it fibromyalgia. Fibromyalgia is a systemic illness that has no known cure. Doctors are only able to lessen its symptoms. It is categorized as excruciating trigger points of pain in the body.

I know from experience that fibromyalgia is an overload of emotional as well as physical toxins in the body. People need to find a way to release the emotional pain that the body is storing as stagnant energy. A way to help yourself is by thinking of the body as an ever fluid river of energy. Visualize pouring pure clean energy into the body through the top of the head. See it washing through.

Reiki is a form of washing the energy out. The facilitator is using their hands as a way to draw energy through their hands, magnifying it, and infusing healing energy back into the body. Some people don't like the Reiki experience. They get agitated instead of relieved. That is because before they can handle more energy they need to remove the stagnant emotional energy that is causing dis-ease.

One day, a client came to me with excruciating pain so unbearable that she couldn't be touched. I sat next to her and said very matter-of-factly that she was gang raped in a past life. She just looked at me. It took a moment for me to realize that it wasn't a past life but this life where she had been violated. As soon as that realization hung in the air between us, I started to cry uncontrollably her tears. She comforted me as I emoted what she wasn't able to.

It was a secret she had held in the body for many years. After it was released in our session, her physical pain was greatly alleviated.

I had this happen enough times to convince me that emotional pain translates into physical pain eventually if not dealt with. If someone is having physical pain, they need to deal with their emotional issues and clean up their environment as a way of helping themselves. These are a few things that I tell my clients to help them deal with their pain symptoms:

- Remove yourself from toxic relationships.

- Turn off the news. Our bodies weren't meant to filter the onslaught of negative images that bombard us when we watch television.

- Stop partaking in gossip or listening to others' problems.

- Limit the use of computers and other electrical appliances. They emit low levels of electromagnetic radiation. Taking kelp can help the effects of this.

- Wear cotton and other natural, breathable materials whenever possible. This gives the body a better chance to breathe.

- Take perfumes out of your home and environment.

- Take walks in nature, barefoot when possible. Trees have a magnetic healing property. They draw the negative energy out of the body into the earth.

- Listen to uplifting music. Music is fluid like your energy system. Listen to the music that you listened to when you were at a healthy point in your life, and let it remind your body what it felt to be good.

- Be creative! When we're creative, our energy is fluid. Pick up an old hobby that you have dropped. It may be helpful in restoring your health.

- Take time each day to reflect on positive things and to be grateful for life's little blessings. It is a physical law as unbending as the law of gravity that positive attracts more positive. So the more that we acknowledge the good things in our life, the more we facilitate more of the same gushing toward us.

40 TAKE IN GRATITUDE

Get in the habit of breathing in Gratitude as you take in each breath. Gratitude is something that we think of giving out more than taking in. But anyone who has struggled with getting enough air or remembers taking that last breath in a past lifetime, knows what a blessing each breath is.

Taking in Gratitude is a simple but very effective form of healing. It is charging the life force as you take it in and introduce it to your body, so it is also charging your very atoms. It is like giving the billions of cells that comprise you a splash of cold water in their little faces.

41 TAKE OUT PAIN

Here is my secret for dealing with pain. Usually people try to resist it. First of all, go into the pain. When you run from feeling it, you create bigger reactions to it and that creates more pain. Dive into the pain and move your energy through it. Not away from it.

Find the place in your body that is feeling the most pain. Go into it. Then pinpoint the spot in that area that is the most concentrated point of pain. Focus on that point. Then do that again until the pain is in one little pixel of pain in the body. Just one little pinpoint. Focus all your attention on that one little pixel. It is much easier to tolerate.

The pain then is not throbbing all over the place. It is in one pinned down spot. Once it is in one pinned down spot, it is either manageable or it just dissipates because the pain isn't really in the body, it is a brain signal. And by focusing all your attention to the part of the body where the brain's signal came from, you are interrupting the pain signal.

It is a way of taking out the satellite signal for pain. Try this. It has worked for me when it has needed to.

42 IF YOU FEEL THE PAIN OF OTHERS

Instead of taking pain into your body, draw incredible energy into your body through the top your head. Imagine the magnitude of a sun a billion times bigger than ours as an energy source of divine love. Draw it into your body and emanate it out of every pore of your body and into every living being. Sense it dissolving everything that is not divine love. Instead of causing you to implode in pain, your energy will be helping to free all others by dissolving all that is not love.

43 TECHNIQUE FOR CHANGING YOUR DNA

Everything we are is made up of our genetic code. Until recently, it was believed that DNA was unchangeable. But it has been proven that DNA can be changed. Taking that awareness to empowerment stage means there is an ability to eliminate a disease in your family tree. I totally believe that changing your own DNA is a powerful tool for self-healing and empowerment.

How did genetic diseases begin in the makeup of our ancestry? Each disease started as an emotional issue that was so ingrained that it got passed down as a genetic component. Our ancestors started out as genetic clean slates, but through fear and conditioning we altered our human make up.

Here is a technique to change your genetic code. Think of yourself as a tube of energy with a lot of little squares in a unique pattern all over it. They are like tiny windows. Imagine your parents and grandparents as similar tubes of energy with different patterns of squares on them.

Choose the parent that you feel has the most qualities that you like. Think about each quality they have. Visualize the tube of energy that they are being superimposed into the tube of energy that you are. It may look like another tube within your tube. But you can see both at the same time.

Each of the little squares on the tubes represents a quality or trait. Every trait is either desirable to you or not. As your tubes are aligned, go through each trait your parent has. If it is a trait you want to enhance in yourself, switch that square on within your tube. If it is an undesirable trait, like a genetic illness, turn that switch off on yourself and close up the square that represented it in your tube.

Go through all the traits with this parent, and then pull out their tube of energy from yours. Repeat the process with your other parent, grandparents, etc. Go through all that you know about each relative and create the little square windows in your tube with their desirable traits and remove the square windows of negative traits that you share with them.

After aligning yourself with all your family's desirable traits and disconnecting from the undesirable ones, visualize only your tube of energy. Go through all of the traits about yourself. Keep all the desirable traits switched on. All the undesirable traits, switch off. Break traits down into their smallest component to empower yourself even more. For example, if you like being outgoing keep that switched on, but if you don't like the component where you talk too much, switch that off. If there are traits that you want that are foreign to you, know there is a switch for them as well.

It may seem like a silly technique to some. But when it's taken into consideration how little of the brain we actually use, maybe it can make us realize that the research for better health can happen within our own energy system, and not necessarily by ingesting more chemicals. Also, the time you spend on empowering visualizations is less time spent on worry and degenerative practices.

44 SYNTHETIC HAPPINESS

I recently facilitated a session with a client where a huge distinction was made between Joy and Happiness. People are in joy and run after happiness. If someone leaves joy to search for happiness, then happiness is a lie. That is what my client was struggling with.

People think of happiness as the ultimate truth. But happiness can have different grades, like sweetness. There is a huge difference between an organic pear and processed candy. One may prefer the candy, but it leaves their taste buds distorted and not able to taste the organic succor of the natural fruit.

These are the worlds of duality, meaning every positive has an equal opposite. So happy stints will cycle into sad stints. This is the cycle of life. The higher reality is contentment. Contentment is like the organic fruit. It is sweet and pleasant, but we take it for granted and prefer the stimulating rush of the synthetic sugar.

So the problem with happiness is when people come out of their contentment to achieve the feeling of it. Feeling the happiness instead of being happy may be the difference between being grounded and centered and chasing a lie.

Here are some examples:

- Exhausting one's self during the holiday season to manufacture a special day as opposed to enjoying the splendor of each day.

- Having to buy special items to feel happy: shoes, clothes, electronics.

- Being unhappy if things don't go a particular way instead of just being happy regardless.

- Making a new event about celebration instead of enjoyment: weddings, babies, birthdays, etc.

- Needing a special occasion to value someone else.
- Having the news, celebrities, the calendar, or a relationship dictate whether we are happy or not.

If any of this resonates, you may want to do these taps:

(Say each statement three times while tapping on your head, and say it a fourth time while tapping on your chest.)

"I release coming out of my center to find happiness; in all moments."

"I release being whitewashed in happiness; in all moments."

"I release confusing organic Joy with synthetic happiness; in all moments."

"I release using happiness as a form of denial; in all moments."

"I release the glass ceiling of happiness; in all moments."

"I release being imprisoned in happiness; in all moments."

"I release the belief that another person holds the key to happiness; in all moments."

"I release wasting energy conjuring up happiness; in all moments."

"I release confusing feelings and ideologies for happiness; in all moments."

45 TECHNIQUE TO COUNTER WORRY

Make a mental list of some of your favorite experiences. When the mind starts to focus on negative issues, catch it as soon as possible and mock-up a reenactment of one of your fondest memories. Be as thorough as you can with the memory to bring the joy and peace of it into the present moment. Have a running list of experiences handy to draw from. Use as many sensations, positive feelings, and uplifting thoughts as possible.

By doing this, you will be training the mind to be helpful. You will be showing it what types of experiences you want to have more of. The mind wants to be helpful. It gives you worry because it thinks that is what you want to focus on. It is trying to help. By referencing a list of happy experiences, you will be training it to habitually be in joy and peace.

Here are some suggestions to jog the memory:

- A favorite sunrise
- Being in love
- Saying "I love you" for the first time
- Christmas or an equivalent holiday
- A particular snowfall
- A loving interaction
- A time you shined
- A peaceful storm
- A time you were validated
- Holding your child/pet
- Doing what you love
- A wish that came true

- The feel of being near the ocean
- The smell of cut grass
- The warmth of being by a crackling fire
- The satisfaction after a feast
- When you felt beautiful, accomplished or rich
- The last day of school

Stay only in the good part of experiences. Some people have habitually trained themselves to think negatively so they will take the experience to a negative. Run through only experiences that are pleasant. Cut it off in your mind if you find yourself digressing and immediately go back to the beginning of the experience or on to another one. This is about self-discipline and empowerment, not a an exercise in remembering just for the sake of remembering.

It is okay to rewrite the script, meaning, if you are thinking of an experience that started out well but may have ended badly, rewrite the ending so the memory stays positive. It is all about raising your frequency to Joy, Love, Abundance and Freedom.

46 TECHNIQUE TO LET GO OF ISSUES

Many times I will tell people to stretch their atoms as a way to expand themselves and let the issues pass right through them. But this is vague to people so here is a technique.

Imagine yourself as a baseball field and all the players are the atoms of your body. All the players are playing close to the infield. So you command them to back up and go out as far as they can in the field. They will be able to catch potential home runs this way.

But in this case, you want the issues to pass right through them. You don't want them to catch anything. You want them to loosen their grip so the issues pass right through.

Now back up your vantage point of being the whole field, but not on a linear plane. Get a sense of all the stagnant energy which you can visualize as a onslaught of uncaught balls, slipping through the hands of the players.

If any issue keeps coming back up for you, try this technique to let it go. It doesn't matter if it is physical, emotional, mental or even replaying the tapes of an uncomfortable experience. Let all issues pass through.

47 THINGS THAT CREATE STRESS

- Trying to micromanage situations.
- The belief that you need to help everyone.
- The belief that you need to be a sounding board for everyone.
- Trying to be "good" or "perfect."
- Neglecting your own affairs.
- Creating business as a form of feeling alive.
- Fear of being alone or empty.
- Creating an identity out of being needed.
- Partaking in groups that create enemies where there are none.
- Living in fear of the future catastrophe.

Fear, control and pride may be preventing you from contentment. Do a scan of your life and look at the things that aren't serving you well. Decide to relinquish them. When disease hits, people are forced to shift priorities. You can shift your priorities before it comes to that.

48 TECHNIQUES TO MAKE LIFE MANAGEABLE

Please visualize containing within you (like stacking cups) all the people, animals, things and intangibles that you dearly love and support. Do this so they do not rotate around each other but are all aligned within you. This way, they are all centered in an infinite love that perpetually nurtures all creation through your love for them and all.

Visualize loving energy bombarding you on all sides as if you were going through a car wash and saturating you with divine love. Don't merely visualize it pouring into the top of your head from an infinite source. This is now too limiting. See Divine Love saturating all aspects of your personal realm with a pulsing, vibrant, perpetual Love.

See all that you love drenched, nurtured and satiated with divine love. Now walk through your day knowing all the world will be enhanced and made lighter by the confidence of your dynamic Love.

49 TENDING TO A ZEN GARDEN

In any of my healing sessions, the client is pulled out of their current vantage point and given an overview of their problems. Once lifted out, they are less apt to overanalyze or react emotionally. Change can then occur. By dislodging the client from strong opinions and emotions, positive healing energy can flow through. In a similar way, a Zen garden heals by taking an individual out of their particular vantage point on earth.

A Zen garden on the surface seems very simplistic. Yet it is a very powerful tool for healing. It is a metaphysical principle that when you heal yourself, you heal the whole. This concept is conveyed through the microcosm (physical self) being a reflection of the macrocosm (Universe). Another way to say this is, *as above, so below.* The Zen Garden is a model of our life, our world, and the Universe.

In a Zen Garden, the rocks represent landmasses and the sand represents the water. The other components of the garden are a rake and a defined boundary. There are layers upon layers of ways to contemplate small Zen gardens using the simple process of raking the sand. One main point is that the garden, like all problems, is contained. The problems are not bigger than the keeper of the garden. The rake is symbolic in tending to problems by humbly infusing them with Love in a detached way.

One of the difficulties in healing is the individual's inability to let go of a problem. The best way to heal any situation is by detaching from it. That is the purpose of the simple prayer "Thy will be done." The tiny mechanism of the human brain is incapable of manufacturing the miracles that the Universe is able to. It needs to let go of them so that the Universe can cleanse itself. If a person needs to hang onto a problem, the Universe in its humility, will allow the problem to exist only if it is to teach someone how to finally overcome it. So in a sense, all problems are an exercise in detaching from them. That is simply what a miracle is. It is the microcosm stepping back long enough for the macrocosm to bring order.

So the purpose of the Zen garden is very simplistic but very complex. It is a means of occupying the physical, emotional and mental components of an individual so that the spiritual aspect can come into play and create order. It teaches detachment. This is the way healing is done. The oil spill, for example, was not helped one iota by the fear, anger, and complaining that was spewed in its name.

One can only imagine how much better any situation would mend itself if everyone who had the awareness to do so would redirect their thought streams into loving the planet. They can do this more readily by simply tending a Zen garden with Love for a few minutes a day. It would assist not only in clearing out the individual, but also in creating a conduit for the Holy Spirit to move through and heal the earth.

A great healing technique is to rake the sand, and put love into the process of tending it. See yourself not as one insignificant person, but a keeper of the planet. Know that you are breaking up negativity by lovingly tending to the garden. Rake love into your garden. Remove all judgments and just tend the garden in simple reverence.

Do this as a discipline, not to look for change but to come to a better understanding of the purpose of life. See yourself as a humble guardian of something greater than your human understanding. You may begin to perceive yourself as a watchful observer of humanity. By doing so, you will be on the precipice of Wisdom, Humility and Healing.

50 HEALING TECHNIQUE FOR THE PLANET

A good technique would be to program your bath water with a particular intention. When taking a bath, visualize all your love, gratitude and positive intentions into the water. Visualize sending it back out into the world as a loving force to uplift all the other water it comes into contact with.

Send Love to every ocean, lake, river and stream. There is no ceiling on how great you can make your love. Expand your vantage point from out into space and infuse all the water on the planet with luminescent Love. See it vibrate at such a high frequency that angels can taste its purity.

Your pure intention can and does uplift all of humanity. Know that all humanity is drinking in your love.

51 THE MELTING CRAYON TECHNIQUE

In contemplation, see all the people of the world as crayons of different sizes, thicknesses, and colors. Take them and put them all in a can of clear melted wax. Watch them all melt. But instead of making the clear wax murky, they all immerse into clarity. The clear wax is divine love.

Visualize everyone melting into divine love.

52 BEAUTIFUL GLOWING VIOLET EMBER OF LOVE

Technique: In morning meditation or prayer, feel the Love and Gratitude show itself as a violet glow that looks like a gentle flame saturating your heart and ebbing out to include your whole essence.

As you go through the day and connect to others through a smile, kindness or "share" on social media, see yourself passing or igniting a violet flame in them and warming their whole essence with Love.

Before you go to sleep at night, visualize the earth with all these little dots of violet flames. Watch as these little dots become pockets of beautiful violet glow until eventually the whole earth becomes a beautiful glowing violet ember of love.

53 INNER BEAUTY AS A REALITY

I remember the day I realized that inner beauty was a tangible thing. I was at a restaurant in the days of salad bars. My attention was riveted on a teenage girl collecting a salad for herself. Her beauty was mesmerizing. I couldn't turn away. But then on closer scrutiny, I saw that she had a crooked mouth, a nose that was a funny shape and clumsy limbs. She was still incredibly beautiful, but why? She looked like an angel to me and it was a bit confusing.

That's when I realized that the term inner beauty wasn't just an expression. As a result, I did years of field study on the subject. I came up with an understanding for myself that may be helpful to others. Apparently, all babies have an innate inner glow. But as they mature, I saw some had it in lesser degrees. I attributed it to their crown chakra (soft spot) on the top of their head fusing closed. Again, at the age of puberty and beyond, many children lost their glow. It seemed like there was a correlation between teens with diverse interests and the energy force. These teens seemed to have the "IT" factor.

Now I believe that inner beauty is the ability to draw upon the energy of the Universe and hold it in the body's energy field. If the body was a beautiful chandelier, it would be the chandelier that was ignited with electricity.

I believe some people draw upon the ethers, funnel it more readily into their glandular system and distribute this energy through their beingness. They ignite the mitochondria of every single cell like little light bulbs. The saturating life force becomes visible because trillions of tiny light bulbs have actually been lit. This is how, I believe, real beauty does come from the inside.

I think if people had this realization, those who do everything they could to be beautiful would go about it differently. They would eat and exercise better, and pray/contemplate/meditate more. Maybe everyone would treat others better. Also, maybe the people that are dissecting their faces and doing other practices that disrupt their body's energy flow, would realize it's counterproductive to their passion of being beautiful.

54 WHY WASTE A SONG?

When you are alone, instead of singing to yourself, why not sing with the intention of singing the song to all the neglected babies in the world of all ages? Maybe your song will reach one heart or maybe it will reach a myriad of hearts. Isn't it a noble cause to use all our capabilities to uplift those who could use our attention? It would seem silly if anyone knew what we were doing, but we can do it all within the confines of our own heart. Who knows, maybe this is how each angel gets their start.

55 RELEASING THE AVERSION TO COLOR

I had a client who enjoyed the color black as her main color. There was no color scheme in her home, and she thought that black looked best on her because it was slimming. But a revelation came that she was stuck in mourning.

It was so subtle and so ingrained that she just thought she liked earth colors and black and white. Once she discovered she was stuck in a grieving mode, she awakened to color and she awakened to her own Joy.

Here are the taps that could help:

(Say each statement three times while tapping on your head, and say it a fourth time while tapping on your chest.)

"I release the aversion to color; in all moments."

"I release being stuck in mourning (shiva); in all moments."

"I release the belief that color is immodest; in all moments."

"I release defining color as arrogant or disrespectful; in all moments."

"I release the belief that colors are disrespectful to God; in all moments."

"I shift my paradigm from black and white to color; in all moments."

"I am centered in a colorful array of Joy, Love, Abundance, Freedom and Wholeness; in all moments."

Color represents different things. To deny color is to deny your own essence. Green is vitality. Pink is emotional balance. Orange is healing. Blue is mental balance. Purple is healthy imagination and yellow is spirituality. They all intertwine and interweave in such a beautiful array to express how dynamic we are!

Energy comes in all colors. If you have an aversion to a particular color, may I suggest that you wear it and get comfortable with it until you uncover the correlation that you are avoiding by not wearing it. For example, red is the color of blood so if someone doesn't like red, it may uncover an aversion to spilling their blood or death.

The taps for that may be:

"I release the trauma of spilling my blood; in all moments."

"I release associating red with dying; in all moments."

or...

"I release associating red with losing my baby; in all moments."

Go through all the colors and see what they connect with. It could be very freeing.

56 TECHNIQUE TO SQUEEZE OUT THE STAGNANT ENERGY

When soaking in a warm bath or hot tub, wrap your arms around both sides of your head and pull the energy down to under your neck. Then wrap your hands around your trunk, right underneath your arm pits and push the energy down to beyond your hips.

Take your hands and wrap them around one leg and push all the stagnant energy out down to the bottom of your feet. Do it as if you are squeezing out a tube of toothpaste. Visualize dark murky energy coming out the soles of your feet and even through each toe. Follow it all the way to the tip of your toes. Do the other leg.

Do the same thing with each arm, only using the one free hand. Visualize all the stagnant energy squeezing out and freeing up your body to allow pure pristine energy to pass through your inner channels and to satiate the body's thirst for energy, Light and Love.

Do this every time you bathe. Do it for your pets when you are petting them and teach it to your children.

57 GIVE YOURSELF PERMISSION

Sometimes people will secretly like the fact that they are getting sick because it is an excuse to clear the schedule, put off deadlines and just nurture themselves. I am wondering how many people manifest real illness as a means to catch a break.

Technique:

Give yourself permission to take the time to rest from your daily routine and just nurture yourself. Do it for a few hours, a day or as long as it takes. Don't talk yourself out of it. The ones who need the break will resist it the most. But give yourself a break, and consider it preventative medicine because it is.

58 TECHNIQUE FOR CONSCIOUS LIVING

Every time you bathe, work out, eat healthy, develop a new skill, treat yourself in some way, you are telling yourself that you are worthy and that you deserve to be loved and cared for. The more consciously that you tell yourself these things, the more effectively the mechanism of your life will run. Love is the oil that lubricates the mechanics of existence. To deprive yourself of Love is a form of suicide.

Every time you tell yourself that you are worthy, you etch it into your energy field and announce it to the world. It is the best way to beautify yourself. And it is also a way to show others who have never experienced self-love how it is done.

59 JUST SHIFT!

Watch the limiting words you put on yourself. You are perfect. Tell yourself that. Let all the opinions, fear, shame, frustration and limiting concepts of you fall away.

Words are the building blocks of our lives here. Don't put it off to the future by saying, "One day." You are no longer chained to this limiting concept of the future. You can shift in an instance.

That is what you can do. The whole Universe is supporting you in doing that. Seize this opportunity and just shift.

60 TECHNIQUE TO BREAK DOWN YOUR ISSUES

I was given this technique in the dream state to share with you. It repeated over and over so it must be a good one for someone.

See yourself not as an individual but an atmosphere in space that has all these particles in it. Some of the particles are chunks of rock while all the others are small uniform particles. The chunky rocks are the problems. There are some big ones and then there are some smaller issues, but they are all mixed in with the regular particles.

As you are looking at the space that is you, simply break down the boulders with your intention. There is no need to delve into them or understand them. There is simply melting them away with your intention so that all the particles within the space of you are even.

This technique could have profound affects in self-healing for some; that is none of my business to know.

61 SAYING GRACE

I always thought it was a nice practice to say grace at mealtime. It wasn't a consistent practice for me. But I have had some experiences that have led me to appreciate the true merit of what I thought was a quaint gesture. Saying grace has become an essential healing practice for me.

It started with an experience I had at a fast food chain. I bought their fabulous chili. When I started to eat it, I went into the experience of watching the beef, as its former self, being led to the slaughterhouse. It was an incredibly painful emotional experience.

I suffered with this knowledge for a while until I realized that I was not a victim of any experience. I had the power to change what I was feeling. So I sat down in reverence and thought about the cow that was haunting me. I visualized going to that cow and doing an emotional release on the cow just like I would do on any client. By doing so, I felt free and more importantly, I believe that on some level I assisted the cow in being at peace.

When the Native Americans were hunting, they would thank the animal that they acquired and honor it. I believe this was their way of saying grace. It was also a way of doing an emotional release on the animal so it could be free of the trauma of being killed.

I would love to be able to be a vegetarian, but I feel my body needs animal protein. So my compromise is doing an emotional release on my meal before eating it. It can be as simple as giving love to all the living items that are being ingested. Also to be grateful for the journey and the process of the meal arriving at the table or drive-thru window.

62 REACTIONARY

When one is centered, they do everything they can to stay in that point of peace. When someone asks them to do something that doesn't "feel" right or tries to cause a reaction in them, they are trying to pull them out of their center. It happens all the time.

When one is pulled out of their center or is trying to defend their stance, they feel like they need a reason. That is creating drama when it isn't necessary. It is enough to say, "I would love to help you out but to do that doesn't feel right to do now." That is all that needs to occur. If others respect you, they will respect your answer. If they don't, then you are being used.

Children are great at needing a reason. When you give it to them, they may launch into attacking it as invalid. There is no need to put one's self in that position. Get the child used to accepting the fact that you may not know the why, but for some reason, what they are asking for does not "feel" right.

It feels awful to be pulled out of one's center. It is like a little knot of anxiety in the body saying, "trust me, don't do this." It must be more horrendous to never know what it is like to be centered. By responding in a non-reactionary way, you are using your awareness to teach others.

63 WALKING INTO ENERGY

Have you ever been in a store or out in public and your mood changes drastically? Sometimes you may be walking into a pool of someone else's energy. If you can catch when you are doing it, it can save a lot of wear and tear on your emotions.

Here is what may happen: You are in a good mood and all of the sudden you get grumpy. Someone else that was grumpy just left the place you are walking through and they left a cloud of their emotion behind. When you walk through, you feel the grumpiness as your own.

Having an understanding of this process, as far-fetched as it may seem, may save you a lot of grief. What we automatically do when we feel a mood change is try to figure it out. We try to label it. Then we react to whatever we assigned as the cause. If we are with our mate, we start to see them as the reason for the mood change and may start problems with them.

The best way to handle mood changes, as difficult as it is for some people, is to not react. If we walk through a grumpy energy cloud and realize that it isn't ours, then we can just walk right through it without taking it home with us. It's a very subtle thing to detect, but by trying, it can make life much easier.

64 HOW TO WATCH TELEVISION

When watching television and movies, pay attention to how music and background noises are used to manipulate our experience. In movies, they are used to draw one in. In advertisements, the sounds are used to imprint the message into our psyche. When commercials are irritating, it is an intentional form of manipulation.

Other ways to manipulate are: Using a person who one identifies with and having them describe their symptoms as if to transfer the symptoms onto the viewer, using fear by showing something horrific and implying that it can happen to the viewer, and using repetition.

Technique:

When a commercial is trying to implant a seed into you, you can feel it as a tightness in the body. Stop it by being conscious of it in that moment. It is fascinating when you realize you can prevent it from coming into you. You can either pass it through yourself into a river of light or send it back to the persons who created the manipulation with a thought form explaining that you don't appreciate being manipulated. If enough people did this, the caliber of television would be different.

I actually send goodwill to uplifting messages in hopes that it will perpetuate more of them.

65 HOW AND WHY TO EMOTE

Have you ever had someone talk to you or felt someone's annoyance with you while driving? Did you start to feel bad? It can also happen when someone is telling you all the bad things that are happening in their life. They are dumping energy on you that they don't want. Many don't realize how habitually they do this, so it starts happening spontaneously when people just are near them.

Try this while you are driving. When someone is annoying you in traffic, instead of sending anger back at them, emote noise, like a throaty little growl. This dissipates the energy that they are trying to push on you. It is processed, gone!

After you realize the dynamic of feeling it and releasing it, you can do it under different circumstances. You can even learn to tune into people's pain and dissipate it like I do. It is a great way to reduce the dis-ease in ourselves, others and dynamics.

Let me hear you roar!

66 TECHNIQUE TO CENTER

Lots of times we feel out of control and we don't know why. When that happens, sit down and make a list of all the things that are causing stress in your life. It is not to put attention on them but merely to show yourself how much you are juggling and that you have a good reason to feel the way you do.

In contemplation:

Sit still with relaxed breathing and eyes closed. Visualize that you are at the center of a solar system. Visualize the planets rotating around you. Are they all in a perfect rotation? Put the planets in a better orbit so that all are aligned and moving in synchronicity. Move anything that is too close farther away from you with your intention.

Notice yourself calm and relaxed when everything is in a perfect orbit and you are centered in the middle of it. Continue to breathe deep and then allow your attention to notice a billion stars all around you. Be aware of the incredible flux of energy that is your core and is holding a center for all these heavenly bodies. Feel empowered.

Return to this state as much as possible. When something else is added to your day, see how it places in your internal orbit. Make certain it is synchronized with your inner landscape. Feel centered, empowered and competent at all times because you are. Instead of running for outer validation from others, go to your inner sanctum and realign your orbit.

67 THE ICE TECHNIQUE

Sometimes we think just because something is in a solid form, it is permanent. But ice melts and so can thicknesses in the body. Visualize the body from an overview. Get a sense where things may be coagulated or lumpy or even cottage cheesy. Just send the intention that everything is melting. Visualize that the thicknesses, callouses, and artery channels are all liquid and running smoothly.

If there is one particular lump, touch where it is on the body with one hand and tap the head and then the chest with the other. This will be telling the brain that dissolving that issue is high priority.

68 SOME HELPFUL SFT

Here are some SFT taps that may be helpful for some.

(Say each statement three times while tapping on your head, and say it a fourth time while tapping on your chest.)

"I remove all the pain, burden, limitations and expectations that adulthood has put on me; in all moments."

"I remove all the pain, burden, limitations and expectations that I have put on adulthood; in all moments."

"I take back all the Joy, Love, Abundance, Freedom, Spontaneity, and Wholeness that adulthood has taken from me; in all moments."

"I give back all the Joy, Love, Abundance, Freedom and Spontaneity that I have taken from adulthood; in all moments."

69 THE RECONNECTION TECHNIQUE

There is a theory I heard that resonated. The reason that some areas in the world are still so warlike is that their DNA is one and a half strands instead of two. Two strands of DNA are the bare minimum for survival. People are supposed to have at least 12 strands of DNA, and 12 strands is our more natural state.

If this resonates, here is a technique to assist the world in overcoming its warlike tendencies. In contemplation, look at the world and see the places that look gray. Then imagine knitting, weaving, or crocheting 12 golden strands where there are two strands. There is no need to direct it in any area. Just visualize creating 12 strands where there are two. Do this in your visualizations.

When you look at the earth again, see if any areas that were gray are now lit up more. Keep the intention of always uplifting the earth with your intention. Whenever you think about it and are in a loving mood, visualize knitting 12 strands together where there were two. Make them straight, even, loving and golden strands. When you look at the earth in visualizations, see it immersed in golden, loving light and saturated in Love.

70 OVERCOMING RAPE

It takes a lot of resilience to overcome being raped. For some people, it affects the rest of their life. Not only is it the trauma. There are feelings of self-doubt, unworthiness, mourning the loss of innocence and lingering fear.

In a recent session, I felt it necessary to point out to my client that more people experience a traumatic sexual experience than experience the fairytale moment that we see in movies. With many, it is between those two ranges, but it is important to point it out. People who have been raped may think that they were robbed of something that everyone else has experienced, and that may not necessarily be the case.

Here are some taps to help those suffering with the after effects of rape. There are so many listed because many people are suffering in silence. My suggestion is that you take the time to do these taps to empower yourself. You are not alone and you are very lovable. If you know of someone who may benefit from these, please share.

(Say each statement three times while tapping on the top of your head. Say it a fourth time while tapping on your chest.)

"I release the trauma of being raped; in all moments."

"I release blaming myself for being raped; in all moments."

"I release the guilt and shame of being raped; in all moments."

"I release the fear of being raped; in all moments."

"I release the belief that I deserved to be raped; in all moments."

"I release the belief I caused the rape; in all moments."

"I release quantifying rape; in all moments."

"I release confusing rape for intimacy; in all moments."

"I release allowing intimacy to be shrouded by the rape; in all moments."

"I release being defined by the rape; in all moments."

"I release mourning my innocence; in all moments."

"I release the belief that I am sullied; in all moments."

"I release the fear of intimacy; in all moments."

"I release the belief that I am unlovable; in all moments."

"I release the belief that I am unworthy of love; in all moments."

"I erase the rape from my energy field; in all moments."

"I remove the rape cookies from my hard drive; in all moments."

"I reboot my system to Love; in all moments."

"I install intimacy software into my system; in all moments."

"I make space in this world for a loving, intimate relationship; in all moments."

"I remove all blockages to having a loving, intimate relationship; in all moments."

"I release sabotaging my love life; in all moments."

"I stretch my capacity to have a loving, intimate relationship; in all moments."

"I am centered in joy, love, abundance, freedom and intimacy; in all moments."

71 TECHNIQUE TO LOVE YOURSELF

The reason that some people don't love themselves is because they can pull up a whole story in their heads of times they felt unloved or mistreated. They make that their reality. They are attached to the story. A good technique to get over that is to visualize yourself without a story.

In contemplation or when you are lying in bed, imagine that you are lying in a petri dish. Simply accept the love, just like the droplets of water. You have no story to wallow in; you are isolated in a petri dish just waiting to accept the love. If water droplets can accept love, so can you. Visualize yourself flourishing into a beautiful crystal.

Everyday while lying in bed, accept the love like a receiving droplet of water.

72 WHEN YOU ARE IN PAIN AND PANICKING

All you have to do is relax. Relax like you have never done before. Distract yourself by doing something you enjoy, maybe even coloring like a child. Relaxing will help it pass through quickly. It is old, old stuff coming out to leave. Don't think about how to fix it; don't think of sad things or regrets. Just relax. Because that opens up your energy, so it can pass through.

73 UTILIZING SELF-ENERGY

Sexual self-abuse is an issue for many. It is considered very shameful for some and is an energetic drain as well. When one partakes of pornography, it is like jumping into a powerful jet stream that is difficult to pull out of. The act of self-abuse can become a compulsion that is neither satisfying nor uplifting. It is a way to deplete the energies of an otherwise efficient person. It can feel debilitating.

Here is a technique to assist in overcoming this compulsion:

There is a great amount of energy that is released during completion. Instead of spilling that away, harvest it to refill the aspect of you that is in need. At the time of completion, pour all the energy that is outpouring back into you. Think of yourself as a child, or when you were most hurting or vulnerable and send yourself incredible love at that moment. The energies that are dissipated will be actually going towards patching yourself up.

This technique may give some the personal strength they need to get themselves out of that jet stream of pornography that they were stuck in. It can also help balance them out so that the behavior or the unnecessary shame dries up. This technique is also great for anyone who wants to uplift themselves or their partner with incredible intention.

74 LOVE IS AS PERMEATING AS THE WARMING EFFECTS OF THE SUN

Love is as permeating as the warming effects of the sun. Everyone and everything indiscriminately absorbs it and emanates it out to all, hopefully just as indiscriminately. So when others inconvenience you by subconsciously being drawn to you, allow them the same detached respect as you'd give a turtle warming himself on a rock.

75 TECHNIQUE TO SATIATE THE LOVE STARVED

In contemplation, visualize the world from afar with all the people of the world as the surface area. See the people who are loved as rounded little domes amongst the masses. See those who are love starved as little divots in the surface of the earth.

In your meditation, visualize pouring love into the earth. Get a sense of how porous it is due to the love starved people. As you saturated the world with Love, watch how it absorbs it similar to how a plant absorbs moisture when you water it. Keep pouring your love into the planet until all the little divots in the world plump up and become domes. Make certain not to focus on anyone in particular. Just pour it into everyone.

If there are any crevices, gullies or receding areas in the earth surface, pour love into all of them. Know that love is not water and you are not flooding the earth with water. Love is love. Water is water. Sense the world plumping up with Love!

76 TECHNIQUE TO DROP THE HATE

You know that feeling of strongly disliking someone? It feels different from loving someone. Think about people you love. Pay attention to how expansive and free that feels in the body. Then think of someone you hate. Get a sense of how that creates a locked up feeling within you. WITHIN YOU!

Take control. It is your energy that is responding in that way. Without thought or feeling being invoked, just change the sensation within yourself from locked to expansive. It is that simple. It is similar to relaxing after holding a breath. It can be that simple. Master your own energy system. You are more than your judgment or your mind. You can love beyond all rationale. Just make the shift.

Once you get a sense of the shift, you can do it with anything. Think of things to react to so you can shift them. It is a powerful tool for being "in Love."

77 TECHNIQUE TO NEUTRALIZE THE "ENEMY"

When we meet someone who we don't like, it is someone who has wronged us in the past. We have a choice whether to make amends and be free of them or to perpetuate animosity and stir up the grudge once again. One of the choices keeps us from transcending and the other is kind, wise and liberating.

The thing about an unpleasant interaction that you have experienced with someone is to look at it from afar, from a neutral vantage point. See the energy around the experience as swirling and tangled while the energy farther away is smooth and clear. Visualize smoothing out and untangling all the energy around the interaction so that it is as clear as the energy that is farther away. When all the energy is smooth and clear, see both parties simply and peacefully walking away from each other in different directions.

78 LOVE ALL FROM WITHIN

There are behaviors that all of us use to protect ourselves. There is the overachiever, under achiever, know-it-all, people pleaser, complainer, the hypochondriac, the addict, zealot, etc.. Some behaviors are easier to be around, but all are merely looking to be loved and secure at the core. It is difficult to do this in our daily interactions because many of these defenses are hard to get close to and the individuals deflect the love.

Here is a technique:

In contemplation, imagine that you are the earth itself. See yourself from the vantage point of being the globe and look at your own body from within. Get a sense of areas that need attention. Send love there and get a sense of the shift. If there is a spot where there is an indentation or bump, send it love to even it out. If the globe looks like a deflated soccer ball, fill it up. Feel your own energy fill up as you pour as much love into the earth as possible.

Continue until you are so full that the love is emanating out of your pores. See it satiating all the living plants, animals and people of the planet. If you start to make a judgment about who deserves it, you have slipped out of the love and slipped into power. Stay in the love. It is the only way to be an effective benefit to others and yourself. Emanate your love out so even the atmosphere is charged with it. Get a sense of it dissolving all that is not love. Offer it to all, and all those who have been deprived, deficient and fearful partake of your incredible gift.

It would be great if you could adopt this visual as a "go to" during the day. When anything or anyone disturbs you, see it as an indicator that the world needs more love and pour it into the world through your visualization. So when someone right next to you is irritating you with their behavior, you can love them from afar. Remember, it is never to change someone. That turns it into manipulation and control. It is only to offer love and respect because you and everyone is love at the core and have the means and awareness to simply Love.

79 HOW WHAT WE THINK AFFECTS OTHERS

Here is an example of how what we think affects others. My dog Simha loves her car rides. It is an absolute joy for her to get into the back seat, look out the window and take in all the sights. She goes from the left back window to the right, and my only job is to keep the chosen window down for her riding pleasure. (At one point, she thought that I controlled the wind because she asked me to turn it down when it was particularly windy.) I take her into most stores and keep a cup of fresh water for her in the cup holder and wait as long as is needed when we get into the car for her to get a drink of water and move to the back seat.

I have a wonderful friend with whom I run errands. She has admitted in confidence that Simha annoys her. Simha likes to be first getting out of the house and this irritated her in the past. I have felt her agitation with Simha and sensed that she was really agitated with me but could not admit it to herself so she projected it onto Simha. But Simha doesn't understand this. It has been palpable. But she is a dear person so Simha and I overlook it.

One day while running errands, my friend seemed particularly annoyed. When someone seems anything to me, others may not even sense it, not even the person themselves. It was very obvious to me and to Simha. As much as this person tried to hide it, she was agitated. Simha was walking on doggy eggshells. When we got into the car after an errand, Simha started to quench a deep thirst. My friend must have been impatient that day and must have sent a very negative thought to Simha because Simha stopped drinking really quickly and ran to the back seat. Her joy was squashed and she remained thirsty.

I asked my friend what she was thinking about Simha. She eventually admitted that she was impatient but denied any particular thought. After that, Simha would not drink from her cup anymore. Through no fault of her own, her joy was squelched. That happened months ago and when I drive with this friend, Simha still will not drink any water. She will look at it longingly but no amount of coaxing will get her to drink in front of this friend. And it is only this friend. I had another dear friend ride with us who adores Simha, and Simha drank happily in front of her.

This is what we do to each other. We become irritated and send out negative thoughts to others and believe our thoughts have gone under the radar. They haven't. The negative thoughts we indulge in are out there diminishing others, crushing their confidence, taking away their joy, and leaving them feeling small and violated. Your thoughts are heard. So the next time you think someone doesn't like you, run through what you have been thinking about them and see if you are not responsible for that opinion by having negative thoughts about them first.

When you go to parties and events, think only nice things about others. Compliment them in your mind with sincere observations. See how it changes the caliber of your interactions. Also, think only nice things about yourself because you are listening, like a third party, to all that you say. Don't do to yourself or others what my friend did to Simha. Allow yourself to continue to drink in the love. It is beneficial to quench that inner thirst that will, in turn, allow you to be kinder to others.

80 OUR BEST WORK

I heard a whimper when I was waking up. I was taken into an experience of a little girl bound and gagged in a trunk. I pulled her out of the body and took her on an adventure in the other worlds. I showed her how grand the worlds were and the part of her that was in the physical body was only a small piece of who she was.

I showed her how to get in and out of the body quickly so she was not trapped into witnessing any trauma that her body endured this lifetime.

Once in awhile now, I go to her and encourage her, kind of like a guardian angel would. When I think of her, it is sometimes her reaching out.

It is good that people are learning the skill of traveling outside their body. The young ones are so adept at this. We play catch up in remembering the skill. Babies come to me in quiet times and we converse in energy. There is a newborn that is an old friend that wishes to see me in the physical. I will oblige.

These are good reasons to awaken with a clear mind. When waking up, don't go immediately into your daily list. When going to sleep, don't focus on what you did in the day. Let yourself go blank and feel with your mind and heart where you could be assisting the Universe. We do so much of our best work in the intangible realms, those of us who are not so goal or ego driven. I highly recommend it.

81 TECHNIQUE TO FILL IN THE VOID

Whenever someone has a need that is out of balance, like a compulsion or addiction, it is tapping into a void that has been created around the energy system of the body. It was created by seepage or accessed through a warped or leaky chakra system.

My mother, way back in the seventies, pointed to a specific spot on her throat one day. She explained that when she smokes, she feels a deep satisfaction at that point in her throat. I have experienced the sensation that she is talking about when drinking sugary drinks. It is stimulating the throat chakra.

Since then, I realized that any kind of craving or imbalance is attempting to balance or even plug up leakage from different chakras of the energy system. Smoking, over talking or eating are ways of addressing the throat chakra. Being addicted to sex is a way to overcompensate at the root chakra. Obsessing over being in love is dealing with the heart chakra.

I followed the energy of a craving in myself the other day. When there is a craving, sometimes it takes on a life and obsession of its own. I was craving something very heavy and savory to "fill me up." I thought I was physically hungry. I ordered a large sub sandwich. I paid attention as the craving in my throat was satiated and the sheer volume of the meal hit a chakra in my stomach as well. But after eating the whole sub in one sitting, I was still hungry.

By doing this, I was able to uncover a helpful technique to deal with the cravings that seem to have a life of their own and can create obsessive behavior. I discovered access to the "void" that exists when one is trying to overcompensate with a vice. I have discovered a way to deal with the feeling of being a bottomless pit.

Through our physical component, the intangible part of ourselves is able to access all of existence. But this capability isn't acknowledged in us as a species. So many people who access these realms do it unconsciously. I see people's chakras as controlled openings into the infinite. But if the chakras aren't working properly, then an empty space is created around the body of the person. It is created by them "leaking into infinity" and not knowing what to do with this energy. It feels like an extension of the self.

This creates a stagnant space of lifeless energy between their infinite self and them in their physical body. The physical part of themselves registers this void of energy around them as part of themselves. It tries to make it more physical by filling it with the object of their desire. When we are craving something, we are trying to fill up the space around us that we have created through a "leaky" chakra.

Technique:

Visualize your own body as an engine to the Divine. See the chakras as gaskets into the infinite realms of possibility. Go through your own chakras and see which ones are warped and not spinning right. These are the ones leaking into the infinite around you and creating a void that you deal with by overindulgence. See your "engine" with all this useless energy around it. It can seem like space around the body that needs to be packed in, or it can look like a huge sack of energy following behind the body like a lawn mower bag.

With your mind and intention, fix all the leaky chakras. Replace the seal on them and reform the opening so that it is no longer warped. Go through each chakra and address the health of each chakra with the same detail as a master mechanic working on a leak in an engine. Make certain every issue is addressed. Make sure every chakra is round, sealed and has a healthy spin on it.

After that is done, you have healthy access to the infinite without the seepage creating void energy around the body.

Imagine the sun as a cotton candy like substance of energy. Visualize being able to pluck out big gobs of energy from the sun and packing it around your body to dry up the seepage and to fill in the void.

As you stuff the energy around the body, notice the stagnant energy fill up with healthy energy. See it return to being part of the healthy background energy of the infinite. Keep doing this until there is no empty space around you. Feel the empowerment that this affords you. Feel the magnetic empowerment of having no abnormal buffer between your energy system and the infinite. Sense yourself returning to being part of the infinite with merely a resilient veneer of energy separating you from it.

Next time you have a strong craving or desire, address the chakra that seems to require attention and go through the whole process of fixing all the chakras and packing in the body with light and love. See how it works to minimize the imbalance. This is a powerful technique to empower yourself. May you access your own strength and omnipotence in using it.

82 TECHNIQUE TO REMOVE THE VOID

Notice how I didn't say "fill" the void. That is something many of us are trying to do. When one wants to eat when they are not hungry, when one wants to shop when they don't need to, when one wants to be with someone just because they are restless and don't want to be alone, these are all ways to fill in the void. But the void could be a cavern into a bottomless pit. There may not be enough experiences to ever fill it.

Next time you feel that emptiness within, instead of trying to fill it with exterior items, take a few moments to try this technique:

See yourself as a orb of light. What does that look like? Is it perfectly rounded and filled with emanations of light and love, or is part of it misshapen, hollow or have cracks? When you get a sense of the orb, reshape it with your intention to be perfectly round or oval. Visualize filling in all cracks by pouring Divine Love into them. Do you get a sense of an evenly contained orb?

If there is a hollow center, visualize a huge syringe and stick it into the orb and suck out the void. (Make certain it is only the void.) Pull out the syringe and empty it into a river of Light and Love. As you aspirate the void, notice the sides, which are made of Divine Love, fill in where the void was. The mind may make a trick of seeing a smaller void there and obsess over it being there. If that happens, just get another syringe that is smaller and has a long nozzle so that you can get all of the void removed.

Make doing this technique an easy go to during the day when you are feeling vulnerable or unloved.

83 SUICIDAL THOUGHTS

Thinking you are going to die or feeling that you are going die are not your organic experiences. They belong to the power energies that are being removed from humanity and are hanging on to any sympathetic soul they can find. Know they are not you. How do I know? Because I had to write this for you so you would stop identifying with those energies.

Just simply unhook them from your energy the same way you would unhook someone who is clinging to your arm. Let them fall away and send them detached love. You do them more good by sending them the love than by allowing them to seek solace in you.

84 DYING TOO SOON

In sessions with clients, I realize why many do not complete tasks. It is because in past lives, they were killed before their mission felt complete. So they continue in this lifetime associating completion with a looming death. Not finishing tasks has become a habit with them.

Try this tap to help ease the procrastination and delaying the completion of goals. Say three times while tapping on the head and once more while tapping on your chest:

"I release habitually putting off completing tasks; in all moments."

"I release confusing completing a project with looming death; in all moments."

85 TECHNIQUE TO LOVE THOSE WHO HAVE CROSSED

If you have lost a pet or a person and want to give them love, send it to them by pouring love into those you have access to. It will be received by the ones who have crossed over by using your tangible connections as a conduit and a surrogate.

Love is not linear so when you give it out, if you will allow, it will seep into every fiber of every being around you, especially when you recognize its nature. This technique is like using your concept of love as a jumping off point to understand and realize the vastness and depth of love.

The ah-ha moment comes when you realize that you don't have to send love or have any intention for it. All we have to do is love and recognize ourselves sitting in a pool of love that saturates every aspect of our own beingness. That pool can flow farther and farther out until you realize that your love is more like a vast ocean that engulfs the whole world and the heavens too.

Also, all reside in your pool of love which is their pool, too. The more others consciously add their intentions to "the pool," the more it will vibrate with Joy. It will expand so that others can dare to consciously Love. This is how all souls everywhere get uplifted.

86 THE GIFT OF SURVIVAL

An aspect of the story of Jesus on the cross has perplexed me since childhood. Why did he have such a peaceful look upon his face? I understand it now.

He withstood the atrocities that the world had thrown at him. He suffered at their hands, but he was not broken. With all the pain and torture he had endured, he remained intact. He was still whole. He had transcended the illusion of the body.

We are able to do the same. Whenever we go through great difficulties that feel like they will break us, being present in the moment of one's own ability to thrive is an amazing gift of awareness. It is the fear of pain, fear of loss and fear of being loveless that defeat people. It is never the experience one is going through itself.

Here are some taps to help you: (Please say each statement three times while tapping on your head and say a fourth time while tapping on your chest.)

"I release being overcome by fear; in all moments."

"I release living in fear; in all moments."

"I shift my paradigm from fear to love; in all moments."

"I shift my paradigm from fear to gratitude; in all moments."

87 THE HEART LIGHT TECHNIQUE

Imagine that we all have a light within. When we are doing what we love, or we are sharing our gifts or simple acts of kindness, our light is shining at full capacity. When we are shining our light, we have the opportunity to ignite the light of everyone we meet.

When you interact with others, you can begin to tell if their light is on or not. Listening, acknowledging others who are overlooked, appreciating the small kindnesses of others, encouraging them to share their gifts or validating them are all ways to nudge their light on.

The goal has never been to have the brightest light to blind others and make them cringe. The goal has never been to have others admire your light at the risk of neglecting their own. The goal has never been to diminish the light of others so that you appear to shine brighter.

The goal has ALWAYS been for everyone to shine. The light of others does not diminish the brilliance of your own. It enhances it. You shine even more brightly when you encourage the brilliance of others.

88 STRIPPING DOWN THE LAYERS

My dog Simha has funny quirks and I just recently realized their origin. Whenever we're in bed, she has to lie adjacent to me; she buries her nose under the covers and when she wants love, she stretches out on her back in dutiful submission. I realized all three of these habits are loving memories of puppyhood. She lies adjacent because that's how puppies line up to nurse, and she buries her head to remind her of the pleasant experience of nuzzling mom. The position of being stretched out on her back is how she lay for mama to receive her bath.

She also has habits that aren't based on loving memories. She'll give a nasty look if someone stares in her eyes; she'll flinch if someone holds something near her head. And she refuses to go outside if it's raining. These habits trace memories and experiences that are painful. They also are very ingrained.

In a similar manner, every single aspect of every single person is a compilation of everything they have ever experienced. We all started out at the beginning of existence as pristine atoms of perfection. As soon as we took form, we started to accumulate habits. They may appear as positive or negative traits, but every single one is ingrained from a past experience.

A great technique in dealing with people is to try to imagine the situations that may cause them to react the way they do. All defensiveness, tirades, manipulation and bragging are the individual's way of using inferior means to express or protect the splendor of the Universal Self.

At the core, stripped of all our defenses, we are all the same. That's what Namaste means. The Divine in me greets the Divine in you. When we exchange a smile, it is actually our infinite self acknowledging the infinite self it sees in another.

By realizing this, maybe it will be easier to deal with those who are heavily laden with layers of defenses. Maybe by recognizing their layers, we can strip off some of our own. It's a great way to learn to greet them with compassion and even gratitude, instead of taking a reactive stance.

89 TECHNIQUES TO OVERCOME LIMITATIONS

Go back and rewrite the script. I was the youngest in a huge, dysfunctional, love starved family. I had to rewrite the script for my brain and body to get the love it needs to thrive. I can love you and I can help you rewrite that script inwardly too. I will be your sister, mother or aunt.

Do whatever you need to do within the realms of your imaginative energy to empower yourself. You are too special to be sandwiched into limited concepts of yourself.

You are strong.

You are dynamic.

You are creative.

You are loved.

You are empowered.

You are intelligent.

You are free.

I love you. Introduce that love into your psyche. See what happens!

90 FEAR OF BEING ALONE AND EMPTY

There is such an innate fear of being alone and empty that people fill themselves with pain and problems to feel full. Being alone and being empty are not the same things.

Technique:

Say this statement three times while tapping the top of your head. Then say it a fourth time while tapping the center of your chest.

"I release associating being alone with being empty; in all moments. "

If that resonates as helpful, do the same process with this statement:

"I fill myself up with the Freedom, Love and Bliss of emptiness; in all moments."

You may feel a lightness right away and a subtle expansion of your own energy field.

91 VISUALIZE LOVE

Did you know that the mind does not differentiate between real experiences and experiences we mock up in our visualizations. Test it out for yourself. Sit in a quiet place and imagine yourself engaged in doing some activity that you really enjoy. Put all your senses into it. Do you feel your heart race a little bit faster? Try it with biting a lemon. Does your mouth water?

This works with everything.

If you are feeling out of shape, visualize working out in your mind and it will strengthen your body.

If you are feeling invalidated, visualize sitting in a room with people you really respect and admire and have them listen to you.

If you are lonely, see yourself at a function where you are having fun.

If you feel unloved, conjure up parents that adore you and visualize them pouring love and attention on you.

This is what fantasy is about--feeding the psyche what the physical does not. Some would say it is not real, but from a certain vantage point the physical is not real. In the test with the lemon and the heart rate, there is proof that it manifests to the physical.

When someone is most dejected, unloved, deprived, and even starved, this technique is sometimes the tipping point between surviving or not. It doesn't have to be used only in severe cases. It can be used every day to empower the individual with what they believe they are lacking. Its effectiveness is limited by a person's imagination and belief system. Even use it to talk to your spirit guides.

92 RELEASE THE EFFECTS OF A FULL MOON

It serves a purpose to be agitated when there is a full moon. It is as if the gravitational pull of the moon on our bodies is gathering up all the angst and agitation that we so carefully dispersed through denial and suppression. It gathers it up into one emotional lump so it can be released. It is the same concept as squeezing a tube of toothpaste to gather it together.

Many humans have lost the connection between their emotions and their physical wellbeing. If they were more equipped to release their emotional angst, there would be less dis-ease in the body. Here is a technique to deal with the emotional anxiety and anger that the full moon reveals.

We usually try to avoid the emotional angst, but in contemplation, feel the angst. See it as a huge pile that is stored somewhere in your psyche. See it as stored in a barn somewhere on your inner property. If it is easier to imagine, see it in the garage. See it as filling the whole barn or garage piled up to the ceiling.

Visualize opening up the doors of the garage or barn. Open them up on all sides to expose the stockpile of emotional issues. Visualize the wind coming through and just blowing them all away. Breathe deep as the wind comes in and flushes the room clean. See how that alleviates the angst in the body. Remember to do this every time there is agitation so that it never needs to fill the whole barn or garage again.

93 THE DREAM CATCHER: LINT TRAP TECHNIQUE

Do you know how dream catchers work to trap the bad dreams from coming into you as you sleep? In contemplation, visualize yourself engulfed in a spherical orb of the same webbing as a dream catcher that you can wear during the day. Make certain that you make it big enough to not interfere with your energy field.

Install it to prevent negativity from reaching you and to draw out any negativity that may be trapped in you. When you are around any negativity, see it collecting on the webbing of the orb like lint. When you are feeling irritation of any kind, see the orb drawing it off you and collecting on the orb as well.

Just like a lint trap of a dryer, visualize pulling off the negativity in a sheet and throwing it away to dissolve in a river of Light. Make certain that you remove the lint from the inside of the trap as well.

94 SPEECH EMPOWERMENT

Gratitude.

Our words and thoughts determine our experiences.

When was the last time you received a compliment and just accepted it graciously? We are taught to diminish ourselves. Even in our self-talk. We are afraid to be perceived as egotistical. But this is just a façade for a deeper fear.

Historically, if someone were pointed out in the crowd, it could mean certain death. One such scenario is the Salem Witch Trials. Anyone could be accused and pulled away from their family and persecuted. This happened in most eras before democracy. Memories of persecution along with many other traumas are stored in our DNA. As much as we may want to be acknowledged, the fear from past eras may be too ingrained to allow it.

The reality is that it's not life and death to be pointed out in the crowd in present times, at least not in America. In one sense, it is a good spiritual practice to empower yourself with self-approval. If things get out of balance, the Universe will bring a blow to the ego to correct it, but it won't be life and death. Also, false humility is a throwback from past lives in sects of worship. To feign humility is unnecessary and smacks of insincerity.

The reason to embrace your greatness is that your mind is on duty 24/7 to manifest what it is told to. You are programming your mind all the time by what you say. If someone says that you are awesome and you diminish yourself, then the mind knows NOT to manifest awesome. It has been programmed for mundane. The mind is a computer so it needs clear instructions. You need to tell it positive things about you all the time. When you do this, you will notice a difference.

Here are some techniques to empower you:

- Stop making jokes at your expense. Your mind does not register humor and will make you a joke to others.

- Take the word "sorry" out of your vocabulary. When you are sorry all the time, you are apologizing for your Beingness. You may be carrying a deep guilt from a past time. It is better to release the guilt and forgo apologizing to the world.

- Say only positive statements about yourself and others. Words are magnets. They will attract like experiences to you. Say positive things to have positive experiences.

- Accept compliments. It is a great way to use another's energy to bring more positive experiences your way. Take it in! If you are afraid of sounding egotistical, you can accept a compliment in an exaggerated way without telling yourself you are a joke. For example, if someone tells you that you are beautiful, just accept it by saying, "Yep, I am so gorgeous!" It is very effective and can be life changing.

- Empower yourself with your speech. Instead of saying "if," always say "when." It is a powerful shift to say, "When I am the CEO," instead of "If I am ever the CEO." By saying "when" instead of "if," you program your mind to work definitively.

- Keep yourself in the moment by taking hope out of the equation. When you hope for something, it puts you in a passive state and holds the desired goal away from you. The same is true of the word "faith." It is better to absolutely know than to hope or have faith.

- Watch how often you sabotage your potential with negative talk. Once you start paying attention, it will make much more sense why you haven't been more effective. You will now be your greatest advocate instead of your worst enemy.

95 INTEGRITY

Integrity is an energetic form of currency that individuals save up, disperse or are deficient in. All forms of currency operate under the same Spiritual Laws of Abundance. Integrity is no different. Energy, like abundance, is our innate state unless we remove ourselves from the flow of it. Maybe if individuals realized how to work with energetic currencies, they would be less apt to feel victimized and recognize the cause and affects of their actions.

One of the biggest ways to create a deficiency in energy and integrity is by not following through with what you agree to do. In your heart of hearts you can have all the good intentions in the world, but if your actions don't carry out your intent, it leaves you weak. It is like your mental energy is walking in one direction, your physical energy is doing something totally different, and your emotional energy is torn deciding which path to follow.

When you make promises you don't keep, those around you quickly learn that you are not reliable. You have weakened yourself. You are like a borrower that a bank won't loan money to. Why should your friends extend themselves to you when you have weakened your own value to return the favor?

When you put conditions on a gift of service it is a passive form of control. It is a subtle form of manipulation. The simple statement, "I will do it when I feel like it," is a way of devaluing the other person and the gift. The agreed task has been downgraded to a manipulative ploy.

Many people trash talk their employer. It is a way of invalidating themselves. How different the work experience would be if workers thought of their service to the company as a gift and also received their paycheck as a gift. The sense of gratitude would change the whole vibration of the experience.

When friends turn away, we as individuals feel like the victim. It is funny how our own deficiencies go unnoticed. It would be a different community if integrity were instilled at a young age. This would abolish the illusion of absolute entitlement for little in return. The community would recognize the power of their own agreements.

Arguing is one of the most ridiculous wastes of energy. It is like children going back and forth on the playground. It is an immature belief that anyone has the power to change another person's belief system.

We argue as individuals, groups, communities and whole countries. It keeps the participants busy so they don't have to deal with their own issues. We argue as a way to prove our superiority over another. It's a waste of energy. The better approach is to silently demonstrate our strength of character by walking in whatever conditions we have agreed to. Our character then speaks for itself.

If you are ever around two people who are arguing, make a point not to be drawn into it. If you are able to view the situation from a detached vantage point, you will be able to see that it is actually two egos in competition for validation and not much more.

Once you are able to catch this awareness, you will be able to prevent yourself from dissipating your own energy by being drawn into arguments. Non-reaction is a great way to put the ego in check and to stand in the empowerment of your own integrity.

96 MISUNDERSTANDING GOD

God doesn't care what you call It, Him, Her. God doesn't need to be praised. It has no ego. God does not want you to feel unworthy. God doesn't "feel." God is everything: Love, Wisdom, Abundance and Freedom rolled up into one experience.

The purpose of worship is to pull you into the experience of God, not to make you feel unworthy. To feel unworthy is to separate you from the experience. God is all encompassing. Anything that hints of exclusion is not God but ego or worse-- the attempt of man trying to speak for God.

Anything that separates you from the Source is not God. All of our experiences, our differences, our lifestyles, our uniqueness are meant to hone our abilities to master Love and Compassion for all. Anyone who disturbs our connection with God will be dealt with. It is none of our business.

God does not need power mongers to police the world. If you want to be more Godly, all you have to do is stretch your capacity to love.

Here are some SFT taps to assist:

(Say each statement three times while tapping on your head, and say it a fourth time while tapping on your chest.)

"I make space in this world for more Love; in all moments."

"I remove all blockages to more Love in this world; in all moments."

"I stretch my capacity to Love; in all moments."

97 THE TUNNEL TO GOD TECHNIQUE

In contemplation, imagine that there is a huge, airtight tunnel that runs from you right into the heart of God. If it helps, you can imagine it inserting right into your heart chakra. But when you go into it, it is big enough for you to walk to God standing straight up if you chose.

Imagine that you have this direct pipeline to God. If you have to believe you are still separate from God, at least imagine that there is a direct pipeline. Imagine now, that the only thing that prevents you from walking straight into the heart of God, is all your thoughts, experiences, feelings and beliefs that are jamming up the tunnel.

In contemplation, step out of the tunnel for a minute. Flush it out with your intention by imagining sending a flood of divine Light and Love through the tunnel to wash away everything. Make certain to get it all. See how doing this leaves you clear access to walk right into the heart of Truth and Love, God Itself.

98 TECHNIQUE TO EXPAND INTO YOUR GOD-SELF

Whenever someone doesn't do something that they know is beneficial, it is because even though they are getting wise council from their own innate wisdom, they hesitate to follow it out of fear. Fear is so subtle sometimes. There is fear of being wrong, what others will think, fear of failing or looking foolish. There are so many ways to sabotage ourselves from heeding our own wise council.

The truth of the matter is that one is never going to gain confidence in trusting their own innate wisdom unless they practice it. If you don't listen to your own advice, that gnawing voice of truth, why would your voice keep bothering? When you don't listen, it is like turning down the volume of your own truth and walking away.

Then we listen to others who seem like they know more. The only reason they may know more is that they are either listening to wisdom more within themselves, or they are using their ego to mock up such confidence. If you turn up the volume on your own wisdom, you will know the difference.

The technique to overcome this limitation is very simple. Imagine that you are a God-being operating a human body. Everything the God-being wants to convey in wisdom and kindness has to work through the limitations of the physical body. This body may still have the fears and awkwardness of being human, but there is the God-being component of it that sees the struggle of the limiting parts and has an overview of how to deal with them.

Your God wisdom would know that you are afraid but would also see how afraid all other people are and put the fear in perspective. Your God part would have less resistance to doing the right thing without fear of failing. God does not fail. God heals, loves and can even redirect the little human body. But it never fails.

This vantage point affords many benefits. The more one thinks, feels, acts and exists at this God vantage point, the more they are tapped into the absolute wisdom of the Universe. Doing this technique is a grand example of fake it until you make it.

Also, if you think it does not work but you like what I write, how do you think I tap into such insights to help as many people and beings as I can? Why are people having dream experiences of me healing them? How can I talk to animals, trees and life itself? I use this technique and stay in this vantage point as much as possible while still being aware of the physical component.

I was pushed to this vantage point by being phased out, in a way, from the world that you enjoy. But all you have to do is adopt the techniques that I share. It is a way for you to have the best of both worlds. Heeding the techniques that I share is an incredible opportunity to stretch beyond your present capacities to an incomprehensible freedom.

Take all the limitations off yourself. From the God vantage point you will be able to recognize what they are. They will feel like little uncomfortable glitches in your energy field, like knots in the stomach feel. Whenever you sense one of them, address it right away and expand further. There are no limitations, especially when your intentions are the most pure.

99 HEALING ANY BODY PART

Your _____ is doing everything it can to help you. It is protecting you, it is stretching for you, it's being used as a storage tank, it's releasing toxins. Please don't expect it to be perfect. Please don't reject it or blame it. Show some respect to your personal boundary and sentry in this world.

Every cell of your body has consciousness. Think of them all as a group of little whole people doing the best they can to help you. How would you feel it someone ignored you, invalidated you or blamed you when you were only trying to do your best? This is what you do to the cells of your body. Then when they are sick, you simply poison or burn them or simply cut them out of your body with no thank you or gratitude. No wonder there are whole parts of your body that are stressed. No wonder going to the doctor is so stressful.

Why not try this technique of loving and forgiving all aspects of yourself? Use this technique on any body part or the whole body. You can use this technique every day on a different aspect of the body. It will help you release the intangible element of disease. It is also a way to help you not feel powerless at the hands of disease. You are in control. This worksheet will give you your empowerment back.

Give it to anyone who is in pain, suffering, harboring a diagnosis, is in treatment, feels powerless, likes to talk about their issues. If you are someone who is in a position to share it with others, sit with them and do the first set with them. In doing this, you are a dynamic healer and a very empowered soul.

Here is to teaching people how to be their own healers.

(Say each statement three times while tapping on your head and say it a fourth time while tapping on your chest.)

"I release melting into the background; in all moments."

"I release the fear of being persecuted; in all moments."

"I release the trauma of hearing my own _____ suffer; in all moments."

"I release the trauma of watching my _____ suffer; in all moments."

"I release the trauma of being covered in pain; in all moments."

"I release the trauma of being covered in disease; in all moments."

"I release the trauma of having my _____ violated; in all moments."

"I release the trauma of being tortured or killed; in all moments."

"I release the trauma of having my _____ pierced; in all moments."

"I remove all vivaxes between my _____ and pain; in all moments."

"I remove all tentacles between my _____ and pain; in all moments."

"I remove the claws of pain from my skin's beingness; in all moments."

"I release the trauma of being scalded; in all moments."

"I release the trauma of having my _____ singed; in all moments."

"I release reliving torture; in all moments."

"I release holding back a wall of sadness; in all moments."

"I release confusing love and pain; in all moments."

"I untangle all the pain from the love; in all moments."

"I strip away all the pain; in all moments."

"I dissolve all the pain into the light and sound; in all moments."

"I remove all programming and conditioning of pain from my _____; in all moments."

"I remove all engrams of pain from my _____; in all moments."

"I remove all engrams of humiliation from my _____; in all moments."

"I remove all engrams of shame from my _____; in all moments."

"I remove all engrams of unworthiness from my _____; in all moments."

"I remove all engrams of persecution from my _____; in all moments."

"I remove all engrams of torture from my _____; in all moments."

"I remove all engrams of rejection from my _____; in all moments."

"I remove all engrams of ugliness from my _____; in all moments."

"I remove all engrams of depravity from _____; in all moments."

"I remove all engrams of futility from my _____; in all moments."

"I remove all engrams of anguish from my _____; in all moments."

"I release the trauma and helplessness of watching my _____ rot; in all moments."

"I remove all engrams of putrid from my _____; in all moments."

"I release cursing my _____; in all moments."

"I release faulting my _____ for doing its job; in all moments."

"I release rejecting my _____; in all moments."

"I release blaming my _____; in all moments."

"I release scapegoating my _____; in all moments."

"I nullify all contracts between my _____ and pain; in all moments."

"I remove all engrams of martyrdom from my _____; in all moments."

"I send all energy matrices of pain into the light and sound; in all moments."

"I command all complex energy matrices of pain to be escorted into the light and sound by my guides; in all moments."

"I heal my _____; in all moments."

"I infuse joy, love, health, and forgiveness into my _____; in all moments."

"I infuse security into my _____; in all moments."

"I appreciate my _____; in all moments."

"I infuse gratitude and resiliency into my _____; in all moments."

"I regenerate my _____; in all moments."

100 THE PHYSIOLOGICAL EXCHANGE OF EMOTIONAL ENERGY

It's common sense that if one drinks a lot of water, they will have to relieve their bladder at some point. But when it comes to ingesting anger, sadness, and other "heavy" emotions, we think that they are just magically transformed. Because we can't see them, we disconnect from the process of relieving them. Yet our verbiage tells us otherwise:

Someone dumped on me today.

I just had to talk it out.

I have to bounce it off someone.

I am taking in everything that you are saying.

We know that there is a need to get rid of these issues. The lazy way is to dump them onto some agreeable soul. This is pure ignorance. People are hurting their friends because they are too lazy to take action to convert the stagnant energy into a more productive form. Of course, some people are in a chronic state and they may need the help of a professional who is equipped to deal with their barrage of emotional energy. But the rest of us should not have to be made to feel guilty by not being a dumping ground for a friend's issues. We should not require this of our friends.

There are so many people who say they love their friends but have to limit their time with them because all the friend does is want to talk about their problems. They will even get angry at the friend who tries to pull back and ask why they cut them off. They are cutting the friend off from a sense of self-preservation. It is a necessary survival tool sometimes.

There are more responsible ways to convert this energy from stagnant emotional energy to something productive.

- Journal – It is a safe and effective way of getting emotions out.

- Exercise – It converts emotional energy into kinetic energy.

- Self Improvement – It is converting negative energy into positive energy.

- Helping Others – The feel-good component will override the resistance that the stored issues will invoke (resistance is stagnant emotional issues that want to stay put.)

Realizing that there is an exchange of energy in every interaction will make people more conscious and responsible as to what they bring to the table. For example, the reason why people get irritable when they are dieting is because all the anger that they stored in the liver is now being separated from the fat they stored and is now re-manifesting. How many overweight people have situations or relationships in their lives that are overwhelming? Being overweight isn't about being greedy for food. It is about needing a base substance of fat to store the emotional issues that are being carried. People are literally eating their problems.

People need to be trained how to treat each other. Sometimes when people secure a session with me, they think they will be dumping all their angst onto me. I cannot allow that. When I try to explain that I cannot process all the emotions that they want to pass over, that I merely unhook them from them and send them away, they feel frustrated and may continue to energetically vomit on me. I consider it rude at some point and, if they continue, may choose not to interact with them in the future. My way is effective. Their way may serve themselves, but it doesn't serve their target/victim – aka friend.

Some people look for horrific things to put on their Facebook pages. They know they are affecting others. It makes them feel important. People know that it feels good to unload on their page because good people are reading and taking it in. They are disconnected from the cause and effect of their actions and just feel the energetic component of it.

If you are someone who people find to dump on, you may want to look at that. It may feel good short-term to listen to someone and make them feel good. But how does it serve you in the long run? Is your life running smoothly? How is your health? I guarantee that many of the people who have fibromyalgia are the caring, nurturing types. I have told a few of them to abstain from nurturing others for a while. Most have been incapable of doing it because that is how their sense of self is being fed.

The next time someone starts to dump, stop them and shift to something neutral. Explain that it doesn't feel good to your wellbeing to listen to their problems. If they understand then they care about you. If they react, they are inadvertently using you for their own wellbeing. If they continue, tell them to please stop and continue to advocate for yourself, even if you have to tell them to shut up. Make the distinction between caring about them but not caring about hearing their issues. If they still continue, you may have to cut them off. Your wellbeing and your sense of wholeness is your first priority. It is your first job in life to maintain your own balance. Your happiness and sense of balance is never on the table as a bargaining chip for friendship. But a friend's respect of your boundaries and a sense of responsibility in interacting with you is on the table. You hold all the cards. Play your hand wisely!

101 RAISING YOUR VIBRATORY RATE

The Spiritual Law of Vibrations states that everything is in constant flux. All matter is either growing or degenerating. Nothing exists in a static state. The only constant is change.

Matter is like a pile of clay on the potter's wheel. It gets built to great heights only to be broken down again to the base. The process continually repeats itself. Creation is brought to the pinnacle of exhilaration only to return to a humble beginning again and again. Yet the clay is not the same; it is more pliable. It is experienced.

Human beings are living, vibrant energy systems. There is nothing within us that isn't fluid. Even our bones, that seem so hard, still grow and bend. The Law of the Universe is that everything is striving to achieve a better level of excellence. The human energy system is no different.

So why do we fatigue so easily? We wear our energy systems out way too early by adhering to practices that don't benefit it. We create dis-ease in our bodies by treating it like a dead machine instead of a living organism. We have denied it every natural form of energizing itself. It needs real food, fresh water, sunshine, clean air. It also needs intangible energy that is gained through contemplative practices and by contributing to life in some way.

Denial about the natural rhythm of living and dying is making this an ill society. If the selfish people in power were taught that they come back to earth again, wouldn't they take better care of earth? If people were taught that they would incarnate again in a house of their enemies, wouldn't they work to have no enemies? If selfish people were taught that they incarnate as their children's children, wouldn't they be more loving to their children to insure their own happiness?

We as individuals can save a lot of wear and tear on ourselves physically and emotionally if we embrace change as a constant. Everything resonates with a vibration. What surrounds us and imbues us are things of a similar vibration to us. If the people and things in our surroundings bring us dis-ease then it is up to us to change the vibrations of our circumstance to have a better quality of life.

If you are around negative people, move away. By trying to conform, you are warping your vibration. People who are negative resonate at a different vibratory rate than people who are positive.

People who are angry and swear and have destructive habits live in fear of different vibratory rates. So they spew their negativity out around themselves to spread the frequency around that they are comfortable being in. This practice has become an epidemic in societal living. It takes a lot of inner strength and courage not to resonate in one big mass of negativity.

I perceive people as notes in a great symphony of life. Many people are out of tune. They may be uncomfortable to be around. People who resonate similarly will find comfort in each other's company. It's the pack mentality.

When you succumb to peer pressure, you are creating discord in yourself just to have the illusion of fitting in. That's why, in your heart, it feels uncomfortable. The thing to know is that it's easier to maintain your original note than to try to resonate as yourself once you have lost your individual tone. It is always much easier just to maintain your individuality.

If you want to empower yourself, there are many ways to do so. If it doesn't feel right to be around people, remove yourself from their influence. Even if they are relatives and you were taught duty. No one has the right to diminish you. Do creative endeavors that you enjoy. Express yourself in creative ways. Be healthy and fit. Muscle cells have a different vibratory rate than fat cells. Fresh fruits have a higher vibratory rate than a candy bar.

Edit all thoughts that aren't positive. Say only true statements. When speaking, use encouragement and honor everyone that you meet. Throw out all those scenarios in your head where you are victimized. Think of the most uplifting person you can and find similarities between you both. Oprah is so popular because she is one of the most dynamic, influential, loving vibrations. Yet it is easy to visualize talking with her. So have an inner conversation with Oprah or with someone else you admire. Just keep the conversation positive.

Performing daily contemplations, meditations, or prayer is very helpful for maintaining your resonance. Positive affirmations and visualizations work great as well. Every tool you can use to suspend judgment is dynamic in building your integrity and uplifting your vibratory rate.

Use positive visualizations during the day. Whenever you open a door, see it as walking into an opportunity. Every person you meet see as the next great sage of our times. The more you use uplifting tools to empower, the less your mind will be on autopilot.

Sometimes the clearest note is the single note. A lot of students struggle with fitting in or being popular. If they could just realize that the way they resonate is unique and a special vibration. They may be a whole note within themselves and not need the experience of being surrounded by others. Maybe by being alone, they can resonate better. They may well be the next genius, artist or humanitarian.

Wouldn't it be great if, as a group and as individuals, we could embrace our unique differences and resonate to such a degree that we uplift each other to the upper scale.

102 NURTURING GREATNESS

One aspect of humility is not finding it necessary to challenge someone's belief system.

When you talk with a child, and they tell you that they are a princess, a great artist or the best at anything, there is no reason to challenge their concept of themselves. Yet we do this with adults all the time. We find it necessary to level someone's concept of themselves so they don't feel self-important. We don't want them thinking they are better than what they are in our minds. The real issue is that we don't want them to think they are better than us.

Technique: Do the opposite. Stop being the devil's advocate. Encourage others. See them as the princess, the teacher , the leader, the most talented. Help it shine forth in all. It is not a weakness in them to believe they are these things, it is a weakness in you in not seeing it. We are greater than we think and when we can see it in another, we can nurture it in ourselves.

103 ANGEL HEALING

When you are lying down and your body is tired, there are ways that you can refresh yourself. Visualize your body as a large group of intertwined filaments of light. Visualize standing over yourself and looking at your tired body as a massage therapist would. Scan your body for the tired spots and see where the filaments have gone gray.

Visualize being able to dip into your body and easily unhinge a group of filaments that need attention. Go to an achy part of the body and unhinge a group of filaments. See them pivot out in a clump but still be connected (similar to how a pocket knife opens). Notice how some parts are gray. Work to unbraid the filaments that are gray.

As you unbraid the group of filaments, see the gray being freed like a bead coming off a knotted string. Unbraid the whole group of filaments that you are working with. As you make individual strands out of the braids, see the gray energy just easily slip off. As you finish undoing the braid, notice how bright the filaments have become. They are almost too bright to look at. As you get to the end, the braid of filaments pulls away from you and goes into its proper position. As you finish the whole group, the whole group pulls away from you and melts back into the body.

Go to another achy part of the body and go through the whole process of unbraiding the filaments, watching the gray leave and the filaments getting very bright and reset back into the body. Work around the body this way. First address issues closer to the surface. Then scan deeper and find areas in the body where you may not feel achy but you might notice the light is dim.

After you are comfortable with the technique, you can visualize working at a deeper level in the body by seeing very small filaments and working at a cellular level. After your physical body is a glowing group of light, you can use the technique for working on your more subtle bodies as well.

When you are standing in a position to work, instead of addressing the physical issues of the body whose energy has a subtle green hue to it, you can concentrate on your finer bodies as well. Work on your emotions by working on your astral body. Visualize the astral body as a subtle group of pink filaments and work on unweaving the gray areas from it.

When all is lit and vibrant, address the causal body where you keep all your past-life records. Visualize it as a subtle network of orange. After that is completed, visualize unbraiding the mental body which will be a subtle blue color. After that, see yourself working on a very subtle body of etheric energy which is a subtle purple color.

If you are bold enough, see yourself weaving your light body which will be a golden-yellow and will blend into more subtle bodies that are subtle but brighter shades of yellow. At this point, there is no gray energy to release. It is more that you become aware of yourself as a being of light and how you are woven together.

After you have given attention to all the golden bodies, let go of your intention to work on them. Send the intention to reverse and see the lightest bodies move back towards to the physical and weave all the different colored filaments into one perfectly aligned body. If you can look closely at the filaments, you will see how the different colors are braided together, including the green for the physical body. But as you look on from a distance, the colors will simply blend into an integrated brilliant light.

Come back to your body and notice how refreshed and replenished you feel. You just gave yourself an Angel Healing.

104 TECHNIQUE TO REMEDY LUMPS IN THE BREAST

Imagine your breast tissue as a bunch of swirling eddies of energy. Little round circles of energy like in a Van Gogh painting. All is moving in natural symmetry. Now with your intention, make sure all those eddies are moving and clear and that the energy of them is moving efficiently through them and through the whole body.

If you sense one of them not moving, send your energy in with a stick and clear out the eddies until they are all moving and clear. Watch the sludge that was at the bottom be stirred up and flushed through. Do this with the tissue in both breasts and continue through the whole body.

Get so good at doing this that you can do all the eddies in your body with one intention. This is a form of self-surgery and dynamic self healing. Make it an intention to do this for yourself every day to gear up your body to release all the toxins that it needs to. Do this so often and so completely that it becomes automatic for you to do this for your body.

You can continue further until you do this with your whole body and the energy around the body and continue until the whole world is swirling is healthy little eddies of energy. This is a dynamic healing practice to do for all. Because when we do for all, we do the most for ourselves.

105 BUBBLE TECHNIQUE

You know how when you are washing dishes, you can tell if there is still soap residue if you see any suds or bubbles? With any situation or environment that you are in that feels uncomfortable, visualize being at a vantage point bigger and farther away from it and blow love into it. It would look just like blowing into a balloon but with sending the pure intention of love into it. Make sure not to taint the process by adding an intention. Just blow pure love, like what you would feel for your child or pet, into the environment or situation.

As you blow, visualize bubbles coming off the situation and wafting away towards divine light and being absorbed into the light. Keep blowing until you no longer can produce a side effect of bubbles. You will really be moving out stagnant energy in doing this. Try it for yourself.

Whenever you feel bad about yourself, you can use this technique to alleviate the feeling or even the mental angst by blowing love into yourself. This way, you can love yourself from afar without delving into the stagnant energy that is causing the dis-ease within yourself. Blow love into yourself until all the bubbles clear out.

This is also a good technique to teach children to empower them in their own feelings, thoughts and behavior.

106 CONTEMPLATION VERSUS MEDIATION

Meditation is a sacred time to commune with a deeper part of one's self. But many people find it difficult to settle themselves to the practice. There are a few reasons for that. Some people are so filled up with their "stuff" that it is almost impossible to sit with themselves. Another issue is that these same practices have been used for many centuries and so, in some of our past lives, the practice of meditation was bundled with unpleasant experiences. Meditation could be linked with starvation (fasting), or other austerities.

For people who don't resonate with meditation, may I suggest contemplation and visualization as well. Contemplation is using the imagination and making it so real that one can walk into it and leave the body through the images that they conjure up. It is using the mind as an active participant and pulling all the senses into the experience. It is using the imagination as a jumping off point into the more subtle worlds.

That is why reading is so important for children of every age because it hones their imagination skills. Anything that we imagine is real in a more subtle form. But when we travel there, it can be as real as the physical world. That is why some dreams feel so real, because the are.

If you are not good at meditation, maybe you want to make up some of your own contemplations by going somewhere that is not in the physical world. One suggestion would be Santa's Workshop which exists on the astral plane. There are many depictions of it in movies and stories. What is great about this is that by going there, you can revamp your whole belief system once you realize that such things of the imagination are indeed real.

If you want to prove this to yourself, make it more conscious. Decide to go to the North Pole and visit. I will even be happy to meet you there. See if you can get to the meeting point with me. I will be in the factory near the dolls.

107 THE PRACTICE OF RESPONSIBLE THINKING

Your thoughts are received by those around you. Have you ever been looking at someone in traffic and they unexpectedly turn and look at you point blank?

If you have opinions about people and then wonder why they don't like you, be assured that they're receiving the thoughts that you believed were private. We communicate constantly on a subliminal level. If you pay attention to people's reactions to you, you will see that this is true.

I was dining in a quaint restaurant during a busy lunch hour one day. It was elbow to elbow. Two young women came in the front door. One was pretty conscientious about her appearance, but she was overweight. She seemed very shy and I could instantly see how self-conscious she was. She was trying to hide herself even though she seemed desperate to be noticed.

I suspended all judgment and made a choice to think only thoughts of how beautiful she was. I didn't do anything differently except squelch all negative opinions and think only positive thoughts about her. She dressed well, had beautiful skin, hair and a pretty face. Moments later, her demeanor changed. She seemed happy and outgoing and was a little boisterous. The change was so drastic that I realized my thoughts were actually being received by her. It was a great feeling realizing my effect on her. But then I realized all the times I had negative thoughts about people. Were they being instantly received as well?

There is a reason some people are touchy and reactive. They are being bombarded by the thoughts of others with no outer way to defend themselves. Imagine how frustrating it is knowing you're being insulted with no means to respond.

The best thing you can do for anyone is to think only kind thoughts about them. The old adage, "If you can't say anything nice about anyone, don't say anything at all" should be tweaked. If you can't THINK anything nice about anyone, don't think anything at all.

A good technique to try is to pay attention to your thoughts. Allow yourself to manifest only good, necessary, and kind things. If you find yourself thinking anything else then imagine a huge chalkboard eraser coming down and erasing it. Or imagine unnecessary concepts dissolving in the atmosphere around you. The population would have a lot less heartache and depression if everyone adopted and practiced responsible thinking.

108 RELEASE BEING ONE'S OWN WORST ENEMY

Are you hard on yourself? Do you habitually indulge in self-derogatory remarks? Do your friends tell you that you are your own worst enemy? Do you seem to be always buried under problems or just scraping by?

Some people are comfortable with a chaotic life because it makes them feel like they are busy. It distracts them from touching upon a calm inside. The calm is terrifying at some level because it is equivocated with a nothingness. Many people have a deep primal fear of being non-existent. Because of that, chaos comforts them.

Here are a few taps to keep from working against yourself:

(Say each statement three times while tapping on your head and say it a fourth time while tapping on your chest.)

"I release the fear of not existing; in all moments."

"I release confusing Peace with non-existence; in all moments."

"I release using chaos to feel safe; in all moments."

"I release confusing problems for security; in all moments."

'I release all self-derision; in all moments."

"I release being my own enemy; in all moments."

"I release hating myself; in all moments."

"I release blaming myself; in all moments."

"I remove the yoke of guilt; in all moments."

"I recant all vows and agreements I have made with myself; in all moments."

"I remove all curses I have put on myself; in all moments."

"I dissolve all karmic ties I have entangled myself in; in all moments."

"I remove all the pain, burden, shame and limitations that I have put on myself; in all moments."

"I take back all the Joy, Love, Abundance, Freedom, Health, Success, Security, Companionship, Peace, Life and Wholeness that I have kept from myself; in all moments."

"I release resonating with chaos; in all moments."

"I release emanating with chaos; in all moments."

"I remove all of chaos from my Sound Frequency; in all moments."

"I remove all of chaos from my Light Body; in all moments."

"I shift my paradigm from self-derision to honoring the self; in all moments."

"I shift my paradigm from chaos to Joy, Love, Abundance, Freedom, Health, Success, Security, Companionship, Peace, Life and Wholeness; in all moments."

"I am centered in Joy, Love, Abundance, Freedom, Health, Success, Security, Companionship, Peace, Life and Wholeness; in all moments."

The more we stop unconsciously treating ourselves as a scapegoat, the more we can honor our own beingness. It is in that sacred space of self-appreciation that we enter the heart of truth and gain an understanding of the omniscience of self-love.

109 REAL TIME EXCHANGE ON NEGATIVE THOUGHTS

Hi Jen! Just checking in from our session last week. I've realized that I spend 99% of my time thinking negative thoughts instead of loving thoughts.

Did you shift that?

I haven't, not sure how. With taps?

No. With challenging every thought?

Oh. Trying to, but I forget.

Whenever you think something negative and catch yourself, say CANCEL!

Ok! I like that technique! I can do that for sure.

Or, when you see negative thoughts forming get an imaginary eraser and erase them. Or, just wipe them away with your mind.

So if I do that enough, will the positive thoughts reveal themselves?

You can train yourself to form positive thoughts. You are empowered. You can stop mid-thought and change it to a positive thought. So it is a matter of retraining habitual behavior.

OK, I'll give it a try! Thanks!

You are welcome! You will actually be using your mind in a different way and giving it a job to keep it busy.

110 HOW TO MAKE DISEASE ACCESSIBLE TO ALL

- Make it a common occurrence by running advertisements about it all through the day with strong offensive visuals and likable victims.

- Talk about it with family and friends as easily as talking about the weather.

- Give it its very own color so that when people see it, they automatically think of disease.

- Honor it with races, picnics, parades and celebrity endorsements.

- Mix it with our entertainment so it is pumped into our psyche when we watch our favorite sports or television shows.

- Make it such a moneymaker that big businesses benefit from it.

- Make it a common occurrence to be dependent on harsh drugs with devastating side effects.

- Continue to pump poisons into the food, air and water systems so that every new generation accepts being poisoned as part of life.

- Become so dependent on the monetary system that big businesses and those who have the most money make decisions for all of society.

- Make it very difficult to buy foods that are not laden with toxins. Make the chemicals taste so good that they are preferred over healthy, nutritious, natural foods.

- Continue to cut down trees which are the most natural and easiest way to pull toxins out of our air.

- Demonize those who value trees and understand their necessity in our survival.

- Refuse to see the correlation between emotional issues and the physical makeup of a person.

- Refuse to see the human system as an energy system. Refuse to acknowledge energy blockages as an early form of addressing dis-ease.

- Continue to erode away natural resources so that people cover every inch of the planet.

- Make eating plenty of unhealthy foods a part of every social event.

- Make a disease more endearing by identifying it with a spokesperson who is extremely likeable like Lou Gehrig or Michael J. Fox.

- Treat victims like heroes so it becomes socially unacceptable to say anything negative about the disease because it will seem to invalidate the plight of those who have suffered from it.

- Make it a feel good cause to abstractly rally against it to distract the attention from the big business that benefits from its survival.

- Demonize natural approaches to healing.

- Demonize God gifted healers as flakes, liars, delusional and thieves.

- Idolize western medicine and those who practice it.

- Accept a fate of burning, poisoning or cutting away parts of the body as a natural process.

- Deny any modality that does not glorify western medicine.

- Program society with such complacency that people resolve to die rather than accept any limitations in the practices of western medicine.

- Believe that disease is inevitable.

- Feel unworthy.

- Use being sick as a sense of belonging or validation.

- Continue to pump as many people into the population of the world as possible so that, in general, the individual is expendable.

- Breed ignorance by attacking anyone who says anything that causes a reaction of defensiveness in yourself.

- Demonize whole demographics so that fear can be used as a smokescreen to keep people fighting and attacking each other instead of the issues.

- Refuse to innovate to cleaner forms of energy because those who benefit from the present forms won't allow it.

- Confuse the issues of environment with issues of faith in some twisted way. Make it so that sincere people who are just trying to do the best for their families are pitted against each other and demonize each other as a form of distraction from the bigger issues.

- Continue on the current path.

111 THE PAC MAN TECHNIQUE

When you are out and about, realize that everyone is just going about their day trying to find love. It boils down to that. Every single person is merely doing things trying to figure out how to get more love. It looks different to everyone so it is confusing. But if you remember just that, it may help you to be tolerant with others.

In the game of Pac Man, the little guys walk through a maze looking for the blue dots so that they can win (that is how I remember it). The whole game of life is people running around in a maze looking to eat the blue dot so they can win. The blue dot is love. They eat up all their experiences just to get to the love. They can't see this because they are in the maze. They don't even know where the blue dot is.

When going through your day, realize that you don't need to find the blue dot. Envision yourself as a big blue dot for others. You don't have to be a little one that they need to look around the corners to find. You can be a HUGE blue dot, bigger than the world, even as big as the sky. That way, everyone can get their needs met at once simply by you being the blue dot.

People have been in this maze of life for so long that once they get satiated with love, they don't know what to do. They try to interpret it as a problem because they have been in the maze so long that they don't understand what it looks like to be out of the maze. So they will be restless or try to interpret it as boredom or even create problems for others.

The way to counter this is by doing for others. Doing for others is a great way to stay in the maze without creating problems to be there. It is an interim experience. After the stage of needing to do for others, which is a major cycle, some realize that they merely have to "be." Being the love, just being present and not needing to act is a powerful way of existing. We are human beings after all. Being is our natural state.

112 MANY OF US ARE SO BUSY

Many of us are so busy giving out the Love and support that we forget to feel it for ourselves. Meditation can feel too overwhelming because of this surge that we are constantly putting out there.

If that describes you, here is a technique:

Just sit with yourself. Sit in a pool of the incredible Love that you give out to everyone else. You don't have to do anything but be aware of the Love that is rolling around within you emanating from you.

The sun doesn't just emanate Light and Heat. It is Light and Heat. It rolls around on itself and there is no doubt that it is at the core a magnificent, powerhouse of Light and Heat.

You don't have to be concerned that you are love, you display it all the time. Just remember who and what you are: a pure expression of Love personified. Let your conscious self feel that and be fed and comforted by the truth of that.

113 TECHNIQUE TO PERPETUATE PURITY

When the television and computer are turned off, and it is fairly quiet, pay attention to the sounds around you. Get the sense of their girth. Visualize what kind of line a sound would be if you were to decipher it that way. The refrigerator may be a thinly drawn line with a fine point pen. A plow in the far background would be a thick line of a crayon drawn on rough paper.

Get a sense of the sounds around you and see if you can feel them bounce against you or pass by your borders. Do they bombard you, bounce off, or blend?

Do you know that when you drop a bunch of ping pong balls together, they will start bouncing at the same height? It is like they all averaged out? It is like this with sound as well. It is like blending different notes of music to make a chord. We do this as people. The people who are into power and control are loud and obtrusive sounds. It is interesting that so many of us that are peaceful stay silent. But we can still be helpful as sound beings.

In contemplation, see yourself as a small globe of pure sound sitting where you are in the world. Look at the vantage point of the place you are in as ordinary except for one round globe of absolute contained purity present in the setting. See your borders as contained. Now visualize you getting bigger and expanding the drop of purity that you are until it fills the entire space. See everything calmed and touched by the purity that is you as you expand yourself to be bigger.

Make yourself as big as the town you live in, all the time having your borders contained but seeing your purity transform everything within your orb into purity. Expand yourself to a whole city. Get a sense of the other pure orbs and feel how much easier it is to expand when there are more of them.

Expand your orb as much as possible while still being contained. If you feel tangled energy come in or chaos, stay at that point and calm it. Try to expand to the size of the earth and encompass the whole world in your purity. If you feel unsafe at any point, just make your orb small again. It is less important to be big and more important to be pure and contained. Make certain not to put any opinions or thoughts on what purity is isn't. The only perception is absence of chaos.

Your presence matters in the world. Your beautiful conscious existence is a magnificent gift to all. The more you see yourself and all in this way, the more that you and I manifest wellbeing for all. This is a much more effective way to benefit all than posting images of atrocities on your social media page. That has the opposite affect. If you want to raise awareness, this is how it is done, by lending your purity to help others find purity.

114 TECHNIQUE FOR USING WHITE SOUND

I am very sensitive to sounds. I feel them. When a car goes by, I can feel it pass by my energy field. When the neighbors are loud, it is like sensitive skin being pounded. Synthetic music can jar the atoms of my internal make-up. It is very upsetting sometimes. I don't think I am the only one.

The sounds of nature are very soothing for my energy. They seem to break apart places in me that have "clumped" and even out the atoms of my body. The birds chattering, the bugs sighing, the frogs peeping, the rain falling, the wind blowing are all sounds that work together to redistribute my atoms so they all have their own space to breathe.

Trees are great healers in many ways. They "catch" all the energies and sounds that enter their magnetic field and direct them into the ground to dissipate them. The sounds may be heard under a tree but they aren't felt as harshly. Each generation gets more removed from realizing the healing benefits of nature because they have been born into fewer of them and are less aware of them.

It is a great luxury and an immense benefit to live next to trees. If one is frazzled, a good long walk in a wooded area would assist in balancing them out on a cellular level. Living in a city is great, but if there is separation from the balancing sounds of nature, the whole system may become imbalanced from this lack of cellular regulation.

A great tool for balancing one's self is listening to white noise. White noise is played in the background to fill one's space with uplifting sound so that the harsh sounds do not bombard one's energetic "skin." Think of it as bubble wrap for the energetic body. It is a great buffer for sensitive souls.

Technique: Choose a background sound that is natural and pleasing but generic. It can be crystal bowls, chanting, or sounds of nature. Play it loud enough so that it is louder than the background noises but low enough so that it can disappear into the background. Put it on continuous play. It will buffer out all the sounds that have been bombarding anyone who is not lucky enough to live in the wilderness surrounded by trees.

This technique has saved me from feeling out of control of my environment. It allows me to stay plugged into the me beyond the five senses. If you have a sensitive child, I highly recommend that you give them this sense of peace. It may help others get a handle on their own sense of wellbeing, maybe even for the first time.

115 SENSITIVE CHILDREN

Some children cry a lot. It is frustrating to everyone. The parent keeps asking what's wrong, but the child just keeps crying. Some children are hypersensitive to the feelings of others. They are empathic. They may be feeling others' emotional pain and not even realize it. They experience an emotion first and then try to label and process it later.

I observed this recently with a neighbor's children. The empathic child is three and her brother is a toddler. He was throwing a temper tantrum. The sweet sister just watched with wide eyes. She then stumbled and fell. Her reaction was over the top. She bawled while repeating that she was very mad. The poor little dear was absorbing his anger as if it were hers.

If you suspect you have an empathic child, it is good to help them sort out their emotions. When they get sad, don't keep asking them what is wrong. They don't know. They just feel. Be matter of fact about it and don't add another layer of feelings on it.

Wait until later when the child is calm. Ask leading questions to bring them to the point of the outburst. Help them understand what they are responsible for feeling and what they are not. This will help them separate what they are absorbing internally from the external reality of the situation. It will also teach them better boundaries.

A technique to use when the child is beginning to get emotional is: Tell them to feel the emotion as if it were a cloud in their belly. Tell them to blow the cloud away. This will empower them and they will most likely become joyful. This technique may be the beginning of them imagining a multitude of techniques to help themselves.

Also, when children see monsters or other scary things, please don't invalidate them. All that does is alienate you from being their advocate in a very real dilemma. They are then left to deal with it on their own. It is very scary.

The better way to handle it is to mock the monsters and say how silly they are. Acknowledge them as real, but strip them of all power. Tell the child that the monsters are really afraid of them. Give them silly names. Explain that the more the monsters are afraid, the scarier they pretend to be. Give the child a flashlight and tell them that the light burns them. You will be empowering your child for a lifetime instead of setting them up to be victimized by unseen forces. This will establish you as their confidant instead of a clueless adult.

116 TECHNIQUE TO COMPENSATE YOURSELF

Think of the thing that you would have liked to hear the most or you needed to hear at one time in your life. It could have been when you were a child or feeling particularly insecure. Realize the words that would have been healing for you to hear, and say them often to your loved ones and those around you. It will be healing for you to hear them as you say them to others.

I tell my Smudge and the other kids, many times a day how proud I am of them. They are very confident that they are loved.

117 TECHNIQUE TO ASSIST SENSITVE CHILDREN

Some children cry a lot. It is frustrating. The parent keeps asking what's wrong but the child may not know. Some children are hypersensitive to the feelings of others. They may be feeling other people's emotional pain and not even realize it. They experience an emotion first and then try to figure out why afterward.

It would be helpful if a parent didn't keep asking them what is wrong. It would be helpful if the parent was matter-of-fact about it and didn't add another layer of feelings on it. When a child is getting emotional, give them a tool to deal with it. Tell them to blow the feeling out of them. It will empower them, keep them busy and bring about physiological changes in their little bodies.

118 THE TEENAGER TECHNIQUE

Have you ever watched a teenager get ready to go out on a weekend day? If you ask them where they are going, they won't know. But they will prepare just the same. Have you watched them talk to all their friends and get excited about an event but not know what the event is? They live in constant expectation of having a good time, meeting someone special or just having something unexpected and wonderful happen.

When we get older, we stop doing that. Or, do we get older because we stop doing that? You can change that.

When you get up in the morning, get prepared to have something unexpected and wonderful happen. Recharge that excitement of adventure that a teenager has. Groom as if you are getting ready to meet someone; expect that phone call or message that is going to send you into the world in an exciting new way. Keep your house clean for unexpected visitors. Re-instill that feeling of expectation that you used to have, may never have had but wanted, or have just seen in others.

Opening up to possibilities in this way is a means of programming life to your order. You no longer have to accept the soup of the day or the chef's special. The universe is a banquet and you are the spoon.

119 HOW TO MEET SANTA CLAUS

There are many worlds beyond the physical. The one that we are most familiar with is the astral plane. We visit this world in our dreams and we go here after we step out of the physical body. When we visit the astral plane, we slip out of our physical body through the top of our head. The world that we are in feels as solid and as real to us as the physical world does. The astral world is a vast place. Anything we can dream or imagine in the physical world is very real on the astral plane.

This is a point of contention for imaginative children. They see things very vividly that we don't see with our cynical adult eyes. They are more in tune with the astral world. That is why their nightmares are so horrific to them. We as adults say that they are only a dream, but to children, the experience is as real as walking down their neighborhood street.

We can use this awareness to our advantage around the holidays. When I am tired of being an adult, I imagine going to the North Pole and visiting the toy factory. It is the most delightful place! If an adult wants to open up to the childlike imagination, all they have to do is repeat the same imaginative visualization over and over while attempting to incorporate all of the senses. After awhile, it will no longer seem so whimsical and may become as real as stepping out your own front door. This is a form of soul travel and is practiced daily by people who want to know their true nature as soul.

If you are a parent of young children, the obvious advantage in the holiday season is that you don't have to dread the question of whether Santa Claus is real. Santa is certainly real and he has a distinct personality. Santa is a hard working man of Nordic ethnicity. He is very wise and doesn't distract easily from his work. The only thing that can get his attention from what he is doing is a child who has come to visit him. His whole demeanor then changes. He lights up with a joy that is contagious. He puts all of his attention on the child at hand as if nothing else exists in the world. For him it doesn't. His purpose is single fold. It is his spiritual duty to validate and love each child that happens upon him. He is the wonderful grandpa of all the children of the physical and astral world.

If you want to rediscover your childlike nature of trust, flexibility and hope, visit the North Pole yourself in daily visualizations or as you nod off to sleep at night. Imagine hearing the bells and hoof stomping on your roof. Imagine going outside and seeing a sleigh on top of your house. Feel the cold and excitement. Visualize what it is like to get into the sleigh with Santa and ride on the night sky. Feel the cold in your nose and lungs. See the landscape before you and the North Pole looming closer. Pull in as many details as you can while filling up all your senses. Go into the toy making department and see all the activity. Drink hot chocolate with the elves. You can draw experiences from whatever you have seen in Christmas movies or other stories.

Make it real for yourself. Better yet, bring your children along. Go as a family adventure every night by setting them up with the visualization before they go to sleep. Do the visualization yourself. Report back to each other the next morning on what happened. The experience may be documented in your dreams. If you do this as a family every night, you will be giving your children and yourself the most priceless gift. You will be teaching them a great spiritual tool and broadening their awareness of themselves as eternal beings. And maybe you just might remember meeting Santa Claus.

120 TECHNIQUE TO "FILL UP" ON CHRISTMAS

Christmas cookies are made of the same sugar, flour and eggs as other cookies, but they are more enticing because they are colored and decorated like Christmas. When people eat Christmas cookies, they are attempting to take in the experience of Christmas. They are craving an experience.

It is the same reason we decorate, shop, exchange gifts and overindulge. Yet many still feel empty during the holidays. It's because the experience they are craving is an inner experience and can only be satiated by a deep inner nurturing.

Here is one technique to satiate the inner craving for Christmas:

During a quiet time, imagine making cookies. Imagine mixing a bowl of ingredients. Instead of just pouring in flour and sugar, think of all the things you like about the holidays and pour them in. Think of all the holiday interactions that conjure up joy. Think of family and caroling, memories and special moments. Pour them all in the batter. Think of a warm cozy fire, snowy lane, eggnog and old-fashioned tree trimming. Everything that could be imagined for your ideal holiday, conjure it up and pour it in the batter.

Visualize cooking the batter and decorating the cookies with frosting chock full of the same imagery as the batter. Eat one of the cookies. Feel all the joy and deep contentment that were imbued in the cookie. Feel loved, warm and satiated to the core. This is the Christmas Spirit that you have been searching for.

As you go through preparation for the holiday, every time you feel stressed, eat an inner cookie and it will help you put more love and joy into everything you do for your loved ones.

121 WAYS TO HEAL YOUR PET'S STRESS

Animals are so devoted to us that they absorb a lot of our stress. They try so hard to help us feel better. Sometimes they try so hard that they develop behavioral problems. They may become needy, want to go out all the time or overeat. Many times they're trying to distract their owner out of their own stress.

Emotional stress is held in the body of pets just as it is in their human counterparts. The diaphragm of the body is a holding tank for stress until it can be alleviated. If it isn't addressed, it floods the body's systems and joints. Eventually it manifests as dis-ease.

When assisting a pet with physical pain or behavioral issues, it's ideal for me to do a diaphragm release on both the pet and its owner. Releasing a pet's emotional stress and that of its owner seems to bring immediate relief to the pet. When the emotional stress has been removed, the pet may suddenly become visibly euphoric. I get many doggy kisses during and after a session.

A lot of times the pet has misunderstandings of what is expected of them. For example, a little dog that is in the care of an owner who wants a dog that protects the house, may unconsciously have a huge burden put upon them. So be clear of your intent for your pet. They know everything you're thinking. During a session, when I tell the owner of a misunderstanding they've had, the pet will usually give them a fixed glare as if to say, "Do you understand now?"

Animals come through many traumas to be with us. The amount of abuse and neglect that they have shouldered in their lives can be emotionally overwhelming. Yet they continue to serve with such dignity and unconditional love. Knowing they are an important part of a loving home is very healing for an animal.

I have dealt with many rescue dogs that have communicated the same question to me, "How long will I get to stay this time?" You can alleviate many of your pet's dis-ease by reassuring them that they will always have a loving home. It seems to be an ultimate concern with many of them.

Please show gratitude to your pets. Remember how special a compliment feels to you. Magnify that feeling a thousand percent to realize how important your words are to your pet. I have been sensitive to people who say that their dear pet of many years is just a temporary situation. They say things like they are just keeping the dog for a friend or that having the pet is just temporary. How sad it seems to me for these sweet souls to spend their whole life without the comfort of knowing that they have the security of a permanent home.

Please thank your pets for their service to you. Please tell them how happy they make you. Sing them songs and put their names in the lyrics. Be as excited to see them as they are to see you. Say and think only positive things about them. They know everything you think. Stop telling their sad story over and over. Animals live in the moment, so allow that moment to be one of Love and Joy! All of these things are things you can do to heal your pet. And if you do them, you may just be healing yourself as well.

122 WHEN PETS GET LOST

When pets get lost, they sometimes go into primal mode and forget about the cushy love and the family that loves them. It acerbates the amnesia when the "parent" panics as well.

To get your pet home, calm yourself down and send loving thoughts to the pet. Remind them of your cozy times and their favorite treats, routine and cozy bed.

By doing this, you can snap them out of primal mode and then they may easily be able to get themselves home.

123 WALKING TECHNIQUE

When going for a walk, plan on staying out all day. Don't plan to turn back until you are limping and exhausted. By doing that, you keep your attention in the moment and on the adventure. The walk isn't all about what you are going to do when you get home or running down a laundry list of issues in your mind. The walk will be about the walk. It will be a more pleasant experience for your walking companions as well, especially the furry ones.

124 TRUSTING YOUR INSTINCT

Most of the time, when I do a session on animals or human clients, I get a similar response. What I tell people rings true with them. They had gotten a sense of what I was saying already.

It seems like a great leap of faith to trust your intuition but the more that you test it out with small things, the more you can trust it on more important issues. You can actually teach yourself to be your own intuitive.

For example, if you get the feeling not to wear a certain garment but you wear it anyway, then you have the experience that your nudge was right. Maybe it was too uncomfortable or the wrong temperature. You can begin to trust your instinct with at least wardrobe issues. So once you develop or recognize your gut feeling mechanism, you can use it on more important issues like finding the right diet, job, or relationships for you.

The mechanism of trusting your heart or gut is infallible. It has no ulterior motive. And better yet, it serves your best interest.

125 WHAT IS POSSIBLE IS INCREDIBLE!

Technique:

Think of yourself as one of those old fashioned safes in a bank with all the abundance in the world inside. Imagine your solar plexus as the big round handle that turns the safe open.

Gratitude and uplifting concepts open us up to allow all the abundance to flow. Complaints, fear and judgments close us up so tight that we feel removed from the flow of abundance.

The good news is that many of us are now recognizing our own power in affecting our own quality of life. What is possible is incredible!

126 THREAD YOURSELF

Imagine that your life is a thread weaving into the tapestry of the Universe. We are all weaving together in perfect synchronicity when we are in the moment. That is how nature and animals weave perfectly together; they stay in the moment.

But when you think about the past, you are creating a loop in your thread. When you worry about the future, you create a pucker in the hem. When you continue to do this, you create tangled energy.

Staying in the moment is guiding your thread smoothly through the Universe.

127 VITAMIN "BE"

You know that list of "shoulds" in your head? You created it. No one is going to know when you scratch one or two off the list. That list is separating you from just relaxing in the moment. Whose voice is the "shoulds" in? Yours? A spouse's? Your parent's? Programming runs deep and carries over through many lifetimes. Maybe a task that seems life and death is a carry over from a past time when many situations were life and death. We are fortunate to be able to rest now.

The challenge in this life is to transcend all our experiences. Glean the golden nuggets from them and discard the rest like ash. Let all the angst that drove you to a revelation blow away. Stop keeping it in effigy with the creating of "shoulds." Introduce yourself to the expansive state of resting in a perpetual moment. See what's possible with the bending of time by staring down its ominous whip.

Learn just to be present, just be relaxed, just allowing "be-ing" to carry you through your day. Being present and having awareness in the moment is like a vitamin to an overworked mind and body. Be kind to yourself and take a "Be" vitamin.

128 PERPETUAL CONTEMPLATION

Everything we do can be done as a meditative or contemplative state to bring more love and awareness into our lives. The key is simply doing it with more conscious intention.

For example:

- When you are bathing, you can visualize washing away negative thought forms from yourself.

- When you speak, you can think of each word as a burst of positive or negative energy that you are adding into the environment. You can speak with the intention of only adding positive energy to the whole.

- When you are driving home, you can feel the communion of all the other drivers and treat them with the reverence of leaving church.

- When you eat, you can visualize the love being extracted out of the food and sending it to all the cells of your body. You can send gratitude back to the sponsors of your meal - the earth and the plants.

- When anything unusual happens during the day, you can treat it like a dream message and interpret its meaning.

- When you are doing something that you don't enjoy, visualize how much worse conditions may have been in past eras and be grateful for the contrast.

- When you are relaxing, imagine yourself resting in the arms of love.

- When someone offers you anything uplifting, see it as a gift from the Universe and accept graciously.

- When you are walking your dog, you can realize how they feel when they are enjoying their favorite pastime and allow the pet the space to enjoy themselves unhindered by control.

- When loving your children, you can imagine yourself as a child as well and realize you are nurturing yourself by nurturing them.

This is a way to make the whole day richer and to enliven the lives of those around us more than we already do.

129 THE STRENGTH OF BALANCE

Many people have a blind spot about themselves. Have you ever seen someone who thought they were advanced in a certain way, but the evidence is to the contrary? Like the auditions on American Idol, everyone thinks they will be the next winner, but some can't carry a tune.

We do this in the opposite way as well. We just don't realize our own strengths because they are all too familiar to us. There is not a person I know who doesn't excel in some way that they are clueless to. I can be mesmerized by someone's qualities and they will never realize that I am admiring them.

If you are struggling, try to look at yourself from the vantage point of a third party. Try to see what that different set of eyes will show you about yourself. There is something amazing about you. Shift your attention from what you see as your problems or weaknesses to what you excel at. I guarantee that it is not mundane to someone who doesn't have that skill.

The simple act of maintaining a balance in one's life is a dynamic act. Please celebrate your own strengths instead of cursing what you see as weaknesses!

130 REGAINING EMPOWERMENT

The concept of power is hardly ever explored, but in actuality, it is what drives most people. Some people associate it with freedom, some are afraid of abusing it and some people treat it as a commodity.

Throughout our past lives, we have both abused power and felt powerless. It is easy to tell which a person is grappling with in this life by their behavior. Those of us who have played the power game and have acted out the scenarios of war and abuse in many lifetimes are interested in nothing more than peace. Those of us who are digging in our heels and afraid of being subjugated either have a fear of losing power or a have a thirst for more.

I think if there were an evil, it would be in using others' fear to manipulate them into giving up what little power they have in exchange for the illusion of having more.

Once someone gives up their rights, it is much more difficult to get them back. Health, peace of mind, and even fresh water were once the norm. But now to have any one of those, we have to work diligently. We have created a society that has given up so much peace in the quest for power. As a group, we have given our power over to modern medicine, big business and special interest groups.

The only means of keeping a sense of self is to pull away from the herd mentality and challenge every custom, law, thought and modern trend. Many people have even given up the ability to do this. As a whole, society is happy to dumb down their ability to think and do for themselves. If this were not true, society would fix education. It would delve into truth instead of turning every news show into a talk show; it would value free thinkers instead of labeling them as strange or crazy and then only appreciating them in hind sight.

Throughout history, people who valued nature and fought against big companies were labeled radicals or crazy. Science documents the consciousness of animals, plants and trees, yet society as a whole refutes anything that interferes with the interests of man. Man is still interested in subjugating others through economics, religion, fear and any means possible. In the larger scheme, man is still a barbarian, only a more efficient one.

In a better society, people would not be stripping the world of everything that is of value and hoarding it for self-interest. Everyone would be of equal value and everyone would value themselves. Children learn the value of their own power through social status, athletic ability and attractiveness. The rich, the jocks, and the pretty people all carry around their golden tickets and the rest of us just fall around them in comparison. Wouldn't it be interesting if the person with the greatest value to society was one who was able to set themselves apart from the crowd by being unique?

The two best ways to avoid being used as a pawn in other people's power plays are to think for one's self and to be one's self. Stop giving in to subtle peer pressure. Share a point of view that is neither right nor left but uniquely one's own. Use your life to express what is beautiful to you. See the beauty instead of being afraid of your uniqueness.

There will no longer be power mongers when all individuals express themselves from their unique points of view gained from their own experience. When we all take back our power, power will be spread more evenly throughout the land.

Instead of rallying against others, realize that they are merely on a different learning curve when it comes to power. You have had the opportunity to abuse power in past lives. This may be their time to learn that lesson now. There is no need to engage them. Just allow them to learn from their own mistakes in their own time.

131 RECOGNIZING YOUR OWN EMPOWERMENT

Here is a cute technique to understand what is going on when you are having extreme feelings that seem to have no reason.

In the world, we all have been conditioned to think of ourselves as separate units with no connection to others. We are meant to believe that we have no loyalties or connections to anyone other than family and those we choose to show kindness to. That we have to know the other people to really care about them. This is not the reality.

In truth, we are all connected. We are not only connected to all other humans but also to all other forms of life. Think of all life as one single body. We are all cells in that body. When anyone sends out an intention to inflict ill will on others, it reverberates back into their life in some seemingly unrelated form. But it is related.

Those who are hell bent on doing harm to others are reacting to actions that they have put out earlier that are coming back around and biting them in the butt. It isn't even karma. It is simply their actions returning. Okay well, that is what karma is. But it is simple and exacting. People who send out negative intentions will get beaten up by their own intentions until they learn to stop doing that. Many of us are tired of waiting.

Because many are tired of waiting for everyone to understand this and do understand that we are all one body, they try to speed up the process. There is a theory out there that you shouldn't help people because they will learn their lessons quicker if they get beaten up enough by life. This is a very callous and limiting way of looking at life. It leaves the whole world in a state of apathy. It is supported by beliefs that you shouldn't help people out of fear of taking on their karma or that this world is meant to be a warring world so don't even try to bring peace. This belief has left us all in a state of apathy.

The Law of Love supersedes all other spiritual laws including the Law of Karma. A lover of life will go into any prison cell to comfort a soul in need. The human consciousness is a prison cell. There are those of us who have come here willingly to bring more love to the whole. More and more souls are returning to this organic way of existing. Believing that we are meant to suffer was merely one last ditch effort to keep us enslaved.

So for those who are feeling anger, frustration, sadness or even pain that is not even yours, think of yourself as a pore on the human body. At that moment, you are sweating out the issues of the human consciousness so the whole embodiment of humanity can release toxins. You do this because of your capacity to love. It is much better to get out of the belief that you are a victim in some way by thinking of it in this way. It is much better to recognize your own empowerment and humanity's capabilities rather than its limitations.

132 TECHNIQUE TO CHALLENGE ONE'S OWN BELIEFS

There are things that we believe that no one can convince us otherwise. At one point, life altering experiences always happened around the same time of year for me so I started to brace for them and wait for them. Things did come, but was I inviting them with my belief? Was I lumping non sequitur together to create meaning where there was none? Or, was I actually reminded of a past life trauma that happened at a certain time of the year and bringing something with a similar impact into this incarnation? Maybe all of these things and more.

But I decided to take back my joy by releasing the belief system that compelled me to dread a beautiful time of the year.

What are your beliefs that are holding you back? Only you can name them. They can show up as a reality and it is okay to release your belief in them. Create a statement to release the belief and do the following tap to do just that on a deep level.

For example: Maybe you believe that the winter brings gloom, so create a statement countering that belief. "I release the belief that winter brings gloom." Then you can state it in a positive. "I welcome the Joy of winter." After you create the statement, say it three times while tapping on your head and say it a fourth time while tapping on your chest. Maybe this is a way to stop building upon past loss and gain momentum with the joy.

133 WHEN EMPTYING YOUR DVR

Empty the programming of the mind as easily as you empty old programs on your DVR. As you delete each recording, imagine that you are deleting an undesirable program within yourself. With each program, delete a habit, fear, problem, etc. Continue down the list with each program. Be creative to name an issue for each program each time. Dig deep.

Every mundane activity and routine that we do out here can be used to consciously relate to our spiritual journey. Everything that we do in our daily life can be turned into a technique to bring us closer to Joy, Love, Abundance, Freedom, Health, Peace and Wholeness in some way. All we need is to use our imagination and the desire to live our spiritual truth. By doing this, we narrow the width between our waking state and our awakened state.

134 UNCOVERING OUR OWN PAST LIVES

Someone asked me how to know what their past lives are. It is a great question since it is more empowering to figure it out for ourselves than to have someone else just tell us.

So here is a homework assignment to help you do that.

First: Make lists of all the things that you are afraid of, all the things that you dislike, including climates, people, customs and time periods, and all your character weaknesses and prejudices.

Second: Cross reference your lists to see what things seem to go together. It may start to stir images or ideas in you of why you have an aversion to these things. These are the lifetimes where you may be holding more trauma and you may even uncover the ways that you have died in the past.

Third: Do the same thing with the opposite side of your life, with all of the things you like. Make a list of the people you are receptive to and the cultures you wish to visit. Look at movies which are time period pieces and feel which ones seem comfortable. Think about the times in history that you could have lived comfortably.

Fourth: Use your imagination:

    Who did you love?

    What did you eat?

    What was the climate?

    What were the customs?

Discovering who we are and who we have been is a great adventure. It is our own personal mystery to unravel. And we are the key.

135 TECHNIQUE TO UNCLUTTER YOUR LIFE

Dreams are a reflection of an individual's state of consciousness. Some dream symbols are the subconscious' attempt to give answers to how to fix the physical life. It is a shame that more people don't use their dreams to help understand themselves.

Sometimes people have recurring dreams of a house or building. Maybe the house is pristine, but more likely than not, the house is stuffed with clutter, dark and dusty. This may be a dream showing the state of the individual's consciousness.

Some dreams may take place in the attic, basement or main floor. The main floor may be what is happening in the daily life. Being in your childhood house is trying to decipher issues that are remaining from childhood. Dreams of being in the attic may be working on aspects of your higher self. The basement may represent issues that you have stored away. If you are ready to work on some past issues, maybe you will find yourself in the basement.

Each individual is the expert of their own dreams. Whatever the dreamer's sense is about the dream is the most accurate gauge of what it means. It is a mistake to go by someone else's symbol dictionary to unlock an individual's dream symbol. One person's experience with water may be totally unique to them. For instance, if one person has a fear of drowning and another has had the experience of being quenched of a deep thirst, then the dream symbol of water would have a different meaning in each instance.

Here is a technique to unclutter your life. In a quiet time of contemplation, visualize the house in your dreams. Visualize going through and opening up the windows. Dust everything off. Systematically go through every aspect of it in your mind and throw out everything that isn't useful.

Clean out each room. Envision the place as tidy and uplifting. Since energy follows thought, you will actually be clearing out old issues from your subconscious that you don't want to look at. You are free to just dump them out. If you have resistance to throwing them out, it is an indicator of an area that needs addressing. This is a more objective way to deal with issues than forcing yourself to relive trauma.

I use similar, yet very effective techniques, in individual sessions. People don't want to look at old emotional issues. They just want to be rid of them. In a session, the client and I clear out their whole state of consciousness as much as possible. Sometimes the client is unable to let go of boxes of old emotional souvenirs. That is okay. At some point, they will be too inconvenient to hold on to. A lot of times, pain will be the indicator that it is no longer worth holding onto old conditioning.

If you are in physical or emotional pain it may be time to clean out your house. One other small point. Sometimes the level of cleanliness in your actual home is a reflection of what your inner house may look like. If you can't seem to keep your home clean, maybe doing the inner house clearing technique may help.

136 IF THE LAUGHTER OF OTHERS IS ANNOYING

If the laughter of others is annoying, try this tap:

(Say each statement three times while tapping on your head and say it a fourth time while tapping on you chest.)

"I release having contempt for my own Joy; in all moments."

137 SOUND WHEEL TECHNIQUE

This is to use when you are around negative music, sounds or people who use negative language. Visualize an energetic water wheel in front of your heart chakra, except it churns sound. Imagine the wheel churning in the negative music or language, converting it into a celestial song. See the celestial music straining away into an infinite strand of a beautiful symphony. Feel the service you are doing in the moment by converting the negative noise into uplifting, melodic Divine Music.

The byproduct of a water wheel is energy. Feel how performing this service is energizing to you and the environment you are in. Instead of being affected by the lower vibration of the vulgar noise, you will be converting it into a sweet song. Know that energy is a byproduct of the conversion. The byproduct is Joy for you, the surroundings and everyone in the situation.

In contemplation, visualize the wheel as big as the earth and convert all the negative vibrations all around the world into a symphony of Love.

138 REPAIRING BOUNDARIES

We are more than a physical body. We are a compilation of thoughts, emotions, experiences and a physical form. These are all aspects of us and have their own specific vibratory rate. A way to look at it is that each one of these components of us has its own "body" that aligns with the physical body in a balanced life. When these other bodies are not aligned, there is an imbalance that manifests in the physical. We have all met people who are too emotional or "in their head." These are two ways to not be aligned.

Here is an SFT tap for this:

(Say each statement of an SFT tap three times while tapping the head and a fourth time while taping the chest.)

"I align all my bodies; in all moments."

There is an outer "skin" on each of our different bodies. In a session, I will help people strengthen and repair their own energy field. This is called their Wei Chi. I have done an SFT tap where we have strengthened and repaired the energy field as a whole. But in a recent session, I was instructed to help the client repair the energy field of each component separately.

Here are the SFT taps that I gave to my client that helped tremendously.

"I repair and fortify my etheric body's Wei Chi; in all moments."

"I repair and fortify my mental body's Wei Chi; in all moments."

"I repair and fortify my causal body's Wei Chi; in all moments."

"I repair and fortify my astral body's Wei Chi; in all moments."

"I repair and fortify my physical body's Wei Chi; in all moments."

"I align all my bodies; in all moments."

"I am centered and infused with Divine Love; in all moments."

139 DON'T FALL FOR IT!

When someone asks you a question starting with "How would you feel if...?" don't fall for it. It is a manipulative tactic to draw you into their issue by making it personal. They are trying to penetrate your energetic borders and make you susceptible to their cause. Don't fall for it. They can deny it all they want or be ignorant to their motive but this is what they are doing.

Most likely, they will try to keep you engaged as a means of using your energy to feed their interaction. Refuse. Simply refuse to answer and politely withdraw all your attention from them. It is the way to maintain your objective without exhausting your resources.

140 A QUESTION ON MAINTAINING BOUNDARIES

Q: *I find your post very interesting on how people manipulate others. How does one stay free of this? I am a teacher and I struggle with trying to please or being easily manipulated by students' wants.*

A: The best way to stay free of manipulation is by tuning in to your gut feeling on every interaction until it becomes habitual to do so. It is an innate ability so it should be easy to relearn. Test it out on small, inconsequential matters and when you get that twinge that something is not right, change your course of action. By strengthening your gut reaction mechanism, you will be better able to tell when you need to change a course in any dynamic.

You are in a great position to teach the children to develop this skill in themselves. Children are master manipulators. They challenge adults with the word, *why*. This is a very powerful word for a child. They learn very easily that when it causes an adult to be flustered, they win. So take the weapon of explaining yourself out of their arsenal.

The next time a child asks you to explain yourself, simply tell them that you don't know how to explain why, but what they are asking just doesn't feel like the right course of action. So get used to saying, "it doesn't feel right." They won't know how to respond. They will actually respect something that they don't understand. They will respect you more for introducing them to it.

So when anyone engages you and you feel them in your psychic space, take a deep breath to align yourself because that person is trying to push you out of your center. If you are centered, the answer to how to maintain being grounded will be given. I was babysitting two children one time where the little girl liked to eat. The little boy wanted a bowl of cereal and she had already eaten. She wanted to eat again, but she was clearly not hungry. She used a go to technique on me. She said, "That's not fair!" Since I was centered, I simply replied, "Food isn't a reward system. It is a means to nurture the body." She was speechless and the challenges stopped.

Also, there is an outer protective skin on our energy field that gets compromised. When it does, it is more difficult to maintain our boundaries.

Do this tap. (Say the following statement three times while tapping on your head and say it a fourth time while tapping on your chest):

"I repair and fortify my Wei Chi; in all moments."

As for being liked, there is nothing more attractive than someone who has a skill that the other does not. By forgoing the need to blend in and by showing your individuality, you will be showing up in a way that others admire.

141 THE HUMAN EXHAUST TECHNIQUE

All the feelings that come to you are not yours. They are only yours if you equivocate them with thoughts, experiences or feelings. When you feel this ominous energy come to you, it is as random as a cloud. Yet because there is little understanding of energy, you try to identify the cause. If you forgo identifying a reason, then you prevent it from anchoring to you. It can pass from you easily.

If you are more aware, you can use this awareness to think of yourself as a human exhaust fan that takes in the cloudy energy and converts it to clean energy or love. You don't have to quantify it at all. Take the human element out of it and just visualize converting smoky energy into love. It can be that simple.

If you practice doing this enough, you will allot it to the parasympathetic nervous system and it will become as automatic as breathing.

142 THE FLASHER TECHNIQUE

Here is another gem that came out of the private group phone sessions.

Whenever you have negative thoughts or feelings that you can't seem to turn off, that is merely an indication that there is stagnant energy present. It is looking for an escape route through your thoughts and emotions. Give it one in a more productive way--visualization.

When you are having uncontrollable thoughts or feelings, just visualize opening up your energy field like a flasher would open up his coat. Whip it open and let all the negativity come rushing out and then quickly zip up your energy again. It is funny enough to remember and to do often.

143 BEING ALIGNED AND BALANCED

Some may think of meditation as a means to overcome having physical or emotional reactions. This may be called mind over matter. A more helpful depiction of what meditation can do is align all the different experiences that a person can have so one is not out of balance.

The way an imbalance manifests is from one being too emotional or too mental. So it isn't about putting unnecessary emphasis on the mind but aligning it with the other experiences of existing.

Here are some SFT taps that may be helpful for some.

(Say this statement three times while tapping on your head and a fourth time while tapping on your chest.)

"I release confusing clinging to the mind with being centered; in all moments."

"I align all my bodies; in all moments."

"I am centered in Joy, Love, Abundance, Freedom, Spontaneity and Wholeness; in all moments."

"I am an infinite expression of perpetual Divine Love; in all moments."

144 BETTER BOUNDARIES

When some people have problems, they try to unburden themselves by bringing others into their experience. These are the people who frequently talk about their issues. This is a very specific demographic. They have become experts in dumping their problems on others. It doesn't feel good to be around these people.

One means in which they try to emotionally pull you in is by trying to get you to see their problem as if it were happening to you. It's very subtle but the questions they ask start with, "How would you like it if…?" or "Can you imagine if it were your…?" The more interest you show, the easier it is to entrench you with their concerns. Most of it is unconscious, but that's no reason for kind people to lay down their defenses and accept it.

These people are master manipulators. They feed on drama and create their own conflicts. They are the ones who strategically stroke our ego. When we succumb to their flattery, we are literally opening up our energy field to them. Energetically, we look similar to a multi-petalled flower unfolding some of its many layers of petals. This is the same as spiritually exposing our underbelly. When this happens, they are able to instinctively sense where our vulnerabilities are and use them to their advantage.

The best way to handle these people is not to engage them. Don't answer their hypothetical questions. Be aware of the cause and effect of how their compliments lead right into getting sympathy for their latest plight. You may have to develop a way to cut them off that feels like you are not being rude. There need be no guilt. This is survival. It's not like you can socially call them out for using these subtle methods. It would only engage them further and feed their desire for drama.

Eventually, you will develop more subtle skills. But until then, they need to sense firm boundaries to stop dumping their problems on you.

The freedom that you will feel from the lessons that you are learning is worth the risk of social awkwardness.

145 TECHNIQUE FOR WHEN YOU ARE BEING INTRUDED UPON

Others try to intrude upon us. It is done many times a day. The goal is to influence us or bring us out of our center. Two areas of discomfort are teasing and advertisements. If there is discomfort felt in the stomach or in the chest, there is a way to stay empowered.

Take the flow of energy that is coming towards you, stop it, and push it back to the sender. It is done this way to show them what they are doing to you and what it feels like. Take it only to the place where it started. They will not consciously understand what happened, but they will get the message and feel the reprimand.

There are anti-smoking commercials that are horrific to observe. They are clearly meant to illicit a reaction. The creators feel justified in the manipulation because they believe in their message. No one is justified in manipulating others. When I start to feel myself reacting, I stop it before it penetrates me and send it back to the creators. Maybe they have gotten the message because I haven't seen one of these ads in a while.

Many years ago I was being teased by a group of teenagers. They were in their element and were being ruthless. As the dominant one made a comment about me, I stopped the insult from penetrating me and it bounced back to him. He felt it. He lost his composure, wilted a bit and the cohesiveness of the mean little group broke up. They dismantled into small talk.

There are other techniques that are kinder. When a person is doing this unwittingly with no malice, there is a better way to handle it. You can create space between your atoms like a screen door, and let it pass right through you. You can deflect all the energy coming at you into a river of Light to dissolve. The main objective should always be to stay centered and to stay as loving as possible.

146 NETWORK OF LOVE

Make your love so big and so pure that every living being in the Universe can feel it. See your love as larger than the whole solar system, stuffed and compacted into your body. And when you say your prayers or do your meditations, acknowledge everyone else who is showing their reverence at the same moment as you. See yourself connected into all the other loving souls who are connecting in that moment. Extend that moment throughout your day and stay connected in a network of love.

147 TECHNIQUE TO STAY HUMBLE

When doing anything for anyone else, put yourself in their shoes and imagine what it takes for them to be vulnerable enough to allow you to assist.

148 TECHNIQUE FOR HIRING SOMEONE TO HELP YOU

It is important not to give away your power in any way. We all have had that experience way too much. So pay attention to the answers to these questions when hiring anybody--from a contractor, dog sitter or health professional--to assist you.

Do you like them? What does your initial gut reaction tell you? Do they talk too much about their own importance? Do they lecture or talk like they are the only game in town? Do they manipulate you with praise or use fear tactics?

If you think about any interaction that happened in the past, your gut feeling was trying to assist you all along. You are your best advocate.

149 HOW TO STAY CENTERED

Stuff as much love and gratitude into each moment, and then the next one will come to you instead of you taking yourself out of the moment to go to it. Think of it as being on an assembly line of life. Life brings you the moments; you don't run after them by thinking about the future ones and you can't run back and perfect a moment that was already boxed up and packed away.

This is the key to happiness. Stay focused on the moment in front of you!

150 WE WOULDN'T LET A STRANGER TALK ABOUT US

We wouldn't let a stranger talk about us the way we speak about ourselves.

Technique:

Treat all negative self talk as you would any other attack against your character and shut it down. See it for what it really is: An attempt by the ego to keep you contained so that you won't venture out of its comfort zone. Once you can make that shift and stop allowing the internal onslaught, a dramatic shift can be made.

151 BURSTING BUBBLES OF ILLUSION

I am confident now of my spiritual prowess and yet know that I am flawed. If dynamic spirituality meant perfection, then I would be perfect. I am not. I am proud now to help debunk the myth that being spiritually dynamic means physical perfection.

Everyone can now relax in the myriad of the beautiful chaotic dichotomies that they are. Being rigid in a hell bent single pointed view of perfection is missing the mark. We dance, cry, sing, wallow and immerse ourselves in blurring the lines of all mental concepts.

That is our sprite-like quality poking a stick at conformity. We are bursting each bubble of illusion as joyfully as popping soap bubbles against the backdrop of a sun filled day.

152 NEW STARTS

If you have adopted a new way of doing something or started a new endeavor, be sure not to bring the engrams (habitual behavior and beliefs) from the old way of doing things into the new way of doing things.

If you are in a new marriage, don't bring the issues of the old marriage into your fresh beginning. If you are having a second baby, don't visit your relationship with the first one onto it. If you are starting any new endeavor, make certain that you don't sabotage it with the engrams of past failures. And if you find a new wonderful spiritual path, make certain that you don't bring all the restrictions and limitations of an old religion into it.

I am surprised at the people who are supposedly on a spiritual path of enlightenment telling me that I am going down the wrong path. These are the same people that a few lifetimes ago would be telling me that I was going to hell. They are not serving the group consciousness of the group by bringing such limited dynamics into the collective.

Pay attention to what those in any group you belong to are saying. Address them if you can. See if they are things that you are agreeing to. Because if you are a part of a group, what the others in the group think, say and do reflect upon you. Don't allow what they think and say to also define you, or worse, limit you.

153 EMPOWERMENT TECHNIQUE

Visualize an infinity symbol of energy with one loop encircling the heart chakra and one loop encircling the head. They depict the symbiotic relationship between the heart and the mind. See them working together and creating an exponential synergy of love and intention. Visualize the loops being even and the energy flowing between them smoothly and effortlessly.

Visualize an infinity symbol between the brain and the solar plexus and one between the solar plexus and the heart. Create a triangle of energy working between these three areas. Feel the synergy between the Love, Intention, the Love and the infinite source of potential.

Use this as a seed to begin contemplation and allow the visual to catapult you into the working dynamics of the energetic dynamics of the body.

154 TECHNIQUE TO HAVE A LOVE AFFAIR WITH YOURSELF

Imagine yourself in a past life of someone you would be attracted to in this life. Allow that person to love you now. Be passionate about it. It is easy to trust that person wholeheartedly because it is you. It is a way to have a love affair with yourself and fill that need for love that seems so ingrained and so hard to fill. Develop a passion for you. It is also a way to balance the male and female energy within you.

155 THE AUTOMATIC SPRINKLER

A friend has become very receptive to the "voice" of her houseplants. She says that they all want her to mist them everyday. So she feels compelled to go around the house and spray every one and make certain that they all feel loved and valued.

They really just wanted to be validated. Since they are communicating on such a subjective level, maybe she could validate them on a subjective level as well. I suggested that when she was waking up in the morning or falling asleep, simply visualize spraying them all with love. That way, she wouldn't have to feel anxious that she missed anybody. It was a good way to keep her energy outflowing so she didn't indulge in negative feelings or thoughts.

This would be a great technique to use during the day. Set up an automatic sprinkler system within yourself and spray out love in every direction to everyone around you. That way, you don't have to think about it and just know that you are giving out the love. It is a way to stay outflowing while you have a busy schedule and never have to feel bad that your family, friends, coworkers or acquaintances are being deprived of what you are capable of giving.

It is a great technique to tune into during those times when your patience is tested. It is a great way to stay in love. There are so many side benefits to this technique. You are realizing how vast the range of your intentions can reach. Maybe your mist can span the range of the whole world. Maybe the mist turns into a steady flow and is able to saturate the world in your love. Also, maybe others will learn from your example and be inspired to turn their mister on!

156 MANY OF US ARE EMPATHIC

Many of us are empathic. We feel the plight of others as if it is our own. If you are depressed or feeling discouraged for what seems like no reason, you may be tapping into the issues of others.

The good news is that by letting the feelings pass or just waiting them out without reacting, you could be helping to uplift others.

Technique: So when you feel bad or depressed, imagine it being like a cloud of something just passing through. Visualize helping it pass through you into a river of Light and dissolving. Better yet, visualize the river of Light passing through you and cleansing you of everything but Love and Light.

The more you do this, the stronger you can become. You may want to ask when is it ever your own stuff. It is never your own because you are pure love at the core.

157 THE SOUND CANCELING TECHNIQUE

There are some of us who feel sound bombarding our body as a physical sensation. It is very frustrating to go into a public place and feel the loud person in the room repeatedly bumping into your energy. Or, listening with an open heart to someone who swears out of the blue and feeling like it is a stab to the ribs. Do they know they do this? On some level, maybe this makes them feel powerful. Some of them are scared and making the most noise just so people won't hurt them. Regardless, the harsh vibration of noise is an issue.

Sound cancelling head phones work by meeting the incoming noise with an opposing noise and cancelling it out. Why not do this within our own energy field?

In contemplation at the beginning of the day, visualize a protective globe of energy around you. Make it thick like a porous glass. Within that globe, imagine it filled with miniscule sound atoms bouncing around at a very high speed from your own beingness. Now see that when sound comes into your energy field, it comes in as atoms of sound which are headed off by atoms of sound in your energy field. See the incoming atoms being knocked out of their projection pattern by atoms in your energy field.

Imagine the sound atoms in your energy field taking down the atoms of incoming sound as an altruistic act of love. See this playing out in your energy field a billion times over. As you go through your day, visualize this dynamic playing out in your energy field. Notice how sound no longer hits you, but there is a buffer field of stillness. Pull up this visual whenever you need this reinforcement. Teach it to the sensitive children and adults in your life. It can save them a lot of suffering and being at the mercy of noise.

158 ISSUES DON'T HAPPEN IN A VACUUM

Issues don't happen in a vacuum. If something is affecting you physically, it is most likely affecting you emotionally and mentally, or visa verse.

Pay attention to what seems out of balance in your life and notice how it may reflect in the other areas of your life. If it is too difficult to tackle the core issue, maybe by working on symptoms, you will be dealing with it indirectly.

For example, cleaning the house may make you feel better and give you the right frame of mind to tackle other areas of your life.

Or, being overweight may be too overwhelming to tackle all at once so just do some physical exercise. Do it merely to feel better in the moment and not as a means as solving all that caused the imbalance in the first place.

159 YOU 2.0

Sometimes when we are at the top of our game, we may experience something that is devastating. It is a crossroads. It may make us feel that we have made no progress at all and that we are in the same old situation that we always seem to end up in.

But what we may not consider is all the strength we have gained since the last time we were challenged. When we are challenged, it is important not to regress to an older version of ourselves. Recognize and celebrate every step on the journey to self-empowerment.

160 EMPOWERED, AWAKENED AND ENLIGHTENED

Breathing Technique:

Visualize your lungs as two thick rounded balloons in your chest. They may feel restricted by the ribs that feel like steel girders. Breathing may be labored by a heaviness in the chest itself.

As you take a breath, visualize the air going into the lungs and igniting them like two white ember sacks. If anyone has ever used an old Coleman lantern, there are two little sacs that are ignited to create the glow that is the lit lantern. They look like little glowing lungs. See your lungs as glowing embers like that of the lantern. These ignite the body like a lantern.

As you breath in, and feel any restriction, visual the little round balloons as having seams in them that expand now as you breath in. These seams create expanded lungs that are at least three times the size of what you thought they were. As they expand, all this crusted debris that was stored in the folds of the lungs and the body is dissolved. The burning embers that you envision burn off the crud. It is the light of your own goodness. You are calling upon it to cleanse the energy of your lungs.

Visualize the chest that felt like a heavy weight now feel light and pliable. It is not sheet rock. It is flexible and cooperative tissue that is responding to the inner light that the lungs are emanating. It is melting as if it were frozen and is now warm and cooperative. The ribs that felt like they were steel girders are now flexible and stretch apart easily to accommodate the lungs as they expand as much as they wish.

Feel the warmth of the whole chest region as so much fresh oxygen fuels an inner light that originates in the lungs. Feel that warmth feed through the body as the oxygen that the lungs took in courses through every pathway to feed all the tissue of the body. Feel the brain awaken in contentment and awareness. Feel the passageways of all the body be widened and flush off all debris. Feel every system in the body working in harmony and synchronicity with all the others. All the limbs are warm and pink and you are contented from within.

Feel all the tissue of the body awaken and become more pliable. See the whole body lit up from the inside by the beautiful generators that the lungs are. See every cell of the body lit up in a similar way as their generator is fed by the lungs. Keep this visual in your mind throughout the day and use it to enhance your oxygen intake.

Thank the trees and the greens of the world for creating the beautiful oxygen that your body thrives on. Realize that not only do you take in the air that the trees create but you also take in the wisdom of the trees with each breadth. Be aware and grateful with every breadth. In doing so, you become able to take in more awareness and more breadth. In doing so, you are empowered, awakened and enlightened.

161 BREAKING DOWN THE EGO

It is painful to admit one is wrong. But that resistance to being fallible is the inflexibility that keeps the ego in charge. It is great to have a good sense of one's self but not an inflated view of reality it may create.

I had a college girl come to me very distressed. She had alienated every one of her friends with no hope of repairing the situation. She was devastated. I coached her through going to every person separately, telling them how sorry she was and what they meant to her. I told her to start with the ones she thought would forgive her more easily. She resisted at first but reported back when she had finished. It was an exhausting but liberating exercise. She had regained a place within the group. It was a personal victory for her.

She also had broken down aspects of the façade that the ego creates. It keeps us separate from others. We believe it is to give us an identity, but it is to isolate us from interactions that may create pain. Yet separation itself creates pain. That may be the crux of life.

Here's a technique to break down the façade that the ego has built up:

Either in a group setting or one-on-one basis ask each friend what it is about you that makes them not want to connect with you sometimes. Ask them what is getting in the way of you both being closer. When they respond, do not listen braced or defensive. Listen to the response and allow their truth in. Do not defend yourself or reject their feedback. Just allow it in. This exercise, as painful as it is, will help break down the defenses that separate you from others. It can create a personal triumph in overcoming being controlled by the ego.

162 LISTEN TO YOUR OWN WISDOM

Think of something that you want to know the answer to. Form it into a question. In your mind, ask yourself for the answer and expect that it will come. Pay attention to the thoughts that come into your mind. The answer will have a different "feel" to it than the usual thoughts. It will come in subtly but serenely.

Once you catch the answer to your own question a few times, you will realize that the questions can get harder and harder and you have the wisdom of the Universe at your fingertips.

163 CHANGING ONE'S LIFE CYCLE

Recently, I had a conversation with a friend who has pretty good health but admits to having panic attacks. It was very easy to hone into why. He is middle aged. In past eras, people did not live as long as in the present lifetime, and they get stuck in that old pattern of "winding down" their life prematurely.

This resonated with him and he explained why. He has a lot of projects and things he wants to do, but his mind always puts him in check and he says to himself, "Why bother?" This is the mind dictating the confines of his life. Since the mind can control levels of different hormones, it is important that the mind not be allowed to shut down our levels of different chemicals to induce aging. Here are the taps that I led him through.

(Say each statement three times while tapping on your head, and say it a fourth time while tapping on your chest.)

"I release being confined by past life cycles; in all moments."

"I release living as if death is looming; in all moments."

"I release being conditioned to grow old; in all moments."

"I release living by the dictates of the mind; in all moments."

"I release aging prematurely; in all moments."

"I release winding down my enthusiasm for living; in all moments."

"I recalibrate my life to exuberant longevity; in all moments."

After my friend did these taps, he felt more relaxed in his body. He felt a tightness and stiffness leave his upper shoulders. It was something that he wasn't even aware was there until it was released. The shifts work at such a deep level that the mind does not know how to refute them. My friend was very grateful.

164 CONNECTING

In the thought patterns of my childhood, I would think that there was nothing beyond the boundaries of the roads I traveled. For instance, I never thought there were homes and towns past my school bus route. I knew there were other communities, but it never occurred to me that the roads I traveled could lead to them. There was a convenient disconnect in place within my psyche to "contain" me.

This may be a similar disconnect that people have regarding their concept of God and the Universe. They know there are different ways to worship, but maybe it never occurs to them that the spiritual road they travel intersects with the road others travel.

More importantly, maybe they can't see that their concepts and beliefs can be expanded upon to include a greater community than just those that directly affect their life. Maybe they can connect all the roads on the planet, but what then? There is always a way to expand the confines of understanding.

Whenever someone thinks that they have an absolute answer, they are like a child who believes that the boundaries end at their understanding. There is an abyss between them and the whole.

Here are some taps to assist:

(Say each statement three times while tapping on the head and say it a fourth time while tapping on your chest.)

"I create space in this world for greater truth; in all moments."

"I remove all blockages to greater truth; in all moments."

"I stretch my capacity to accept greater truth; in all moments."

"I release the disconnect between the microcosm (personal self) and the macrocosm; in all moments."

"I align the microcosm with the macrocosm; in all moments."

"I AM centered and imbued with Divine Love; in all moments."

165 LOVE AS SELF-RESPONSIBILITY

The people in your world rely on the love that you exude whether you and they realize it or not. When you fail to love, you become a weak link in a web of connectedness to all of life around you. Feeling that it doesn't matter is an outmoded and selfish point of view. It is reflected in the depravity of this world. We are all responsible to do our best, to share our gifts and to plug into the Universal love that sustains us all.

It matters very little how many people are in our lives. The magnitude to which our love extends would boggle our minds if we were even able to wrap our minds around it. Just love and know that it maters, not in a small linear way, but as a means of sustaining whole galaxies.

166 HOT POTATO

Pay attention to what you say and do and as you are doing it, ask yourself how it serves you.

For instance, people tell other people about their problems to feel better in some way. Maybe in the past, they got comforted when they were sick or when they shared a problem, they felt lighter by sharing it. So that problem had volume. It was a weight that got passed to another.

In society, we feel compelled to listen to other people's problems. But then they make us feel bad so we share them with others to reduce the weight we took on.

In regard to problems, society has become one big game of *Hot Potato*. A better way to operate is to consciously choose who you wish to listen to. By being the chooser, you stay in your center. If you have to choose staying centered or listening to someone's issues, always choose to stay centered. It is okay to tell someone that you can't listen to them now. Then serial complainers may start to realize that it is a privilege to speak with you and not an entitlement.

If you are listening to someone and you feel your mood shift to uneasiness or even anger, you have just come out of your center. It is okay to stop the interaction right then. If the person respects you, they will respect your boundary. If they don't respect your boundaries, there is no reason to put yourself out for this person.

When someone is telling you their issue, don't allow them to bring you into the equation by saying things like, "How would you feel if that happened to you?" or "Just imagine that." Don't imagine it. You don't need to bring the issue into your personal realm. This is a psychic, maybe unconscious, attempt to transfer their issues to you more readily.

When you listen to someone, stay detached. Don't let your emotions get involved. Be compassionate without becoming caught up in the details. When someone tells me something, I look right through the details to the truth of the interaction. If you focus on the emotions, your vantage point is too low.

Even if you focus on fixing the problem, your vantage point is too low. If the goal is to fix things, the best way to help is by looking at the interaction from such an elevated vantage point that there is no right or wrong. The energies are unbalanced. If you are capable of seeing interactions from the point of view of energy, you can help disperse the energy to their equilibrium just by seeing the whole picture and not reacting to a drama.

Once you experience this, it will click in your mind (and heart). You will want to feel this way of interacting always and to stay above the drama at all costs. It will help the wear and tear of all the components of you: the heart, mind and body. People will see the wisdom of it eventually and stop trying to pull down your vibration with their drama.

167 CONCEDE TO KINDNESS

Instead of storing a reservoir of joy for Christmas morning (that may or may not materialize as planned), there is a better way to experience it. How about divvying up that pot of joy from Christmas morning into 365 smaller pots that get divvied up into 24 smaller pots that all get divvied up into 60 smaller pots.

Why not spend every moment in a little piece of the Christmas spirit? Why not be immersed in joy and goodwill? Why not always have in our minds and hearts what we are going to give? Why not give intangible gifts all year long?

Setting this precedent may switch our attention from racing through time to sequestering the moment to states of gratitude and love. Maybe peace on earth is too big for us to envision. Instead of being overwhelmed by the concept of peace on earth, why not foster a perpetual state of kindness at all costs? Just like the way we sacrifice to buy gifts and make the holidays festive, maybe we can sacrifice in similar ways to instill kindness in our daily existence.

If enough of us adopt kindness in the moment, the vision of peace on earth will not only be believable but will be inevitable. To paraphrase John Lennon, I may be a dreamer, but I'm not the only one. It may sound silly but trust me, you want to be in the world that I envision. So why judge it to be ridiculous or impossible? Why not just concede?

168 EMPOWERMENT IS NOT ABUSING POWER

Many of us have made ourselves ineffective because we are afraid of abusing power. We correlate self-empowerment with the extreme of abusing others by being powerful. Many of us have seen such abuse in past lives that we would rather be ineffective in our own lives rather than risk the chance that we were out of balance without realizing it and harm others.

There is another way to look at it. By NOT claiming our personal power, we allow the balance of power to go out of balance in the macrocosm. The only way that power is going to lose its grip in the world is if everyone reclaims it in the microcosm.

Here are some SFT taps to assist in empowering one's self:

(Say each statement three times while tapping your head, and a fourth time while tapping your chest.)

"I release the guilt and trauma of abusing power; in all moments."

"I release the fear of abusing power; in all moments."

"I release choosing power over love; in all moments."

"I shift my paradigm from power to Joy, Love, Abundance, and Freedom; in all moments."

"I release confusing empowerment with the abuse of power; in all moments."

"I release giving over my power; in all moments."

"I am centered and empowered in Joy, Love, Abundance and Freedom; in all moments."

"I release seeing empowerment as a competition; in all moments."

169 DISCOUNTING ONE'S LIFE

We are the ones who put value on everyone and everything in our life. If we are not happy with something, we are not putting a very high value on it. If we want to be happy, we should reevaluate everything that we are and have. We should go through and take the discount stickers off of everything and that way we will stop dis-counting everything.

170 BLISS AFTER MURDER

I had a revelation about people associating the accelerated heart rate (such as from being scared) with being murdered because those are the kinds of places I go with my clients. Those are the experiences that isolate people and make them think that they are so alone. Because in the instance of being murdered, we are alone. I have a conscious memory of being murdered by my husband in one lifetime. There is a bliss after being murdered that the conscious memory forgets.

Technique: When you are feeling anxious, scared, and are having a panic attack, the belief is that you are going to die. Death is not the end but a doorway to a peaceful beginning. So when you are afraid you are going to die say, "so what" to yourself. In that moment, you are frozen in a state of terror. To pass through that state, visualize going past that moment of terror and into the bliss that ensues. This is a means of removing yourself from that pinnacle experience that is paralyzing you in fear.

See the trauma, fear and horror slipping away as you move towards Love and Light and friends who have crossed over. Feel welcomed and loved. Let the angst dissolve out of your body.

171 DEATH IS THE NEW BIRTH

Many people have an aversion to death, but it can be a beautiful and humbling experience. Helping someone cross over in comfort and peace is the most natural and spiritual thing to do. People get confused between fighting to live and the resistance to death. They are not the same.

When the fight is over, and the crossing is inevitable, choose to spend the remaining time left to honor that person and prepare them for their passing. Usually the person crossing is concerned with leaving loved ones behind. So reassure them that you will be okay without them but will just miss them terribly.

People have so many misunderstandings about what happens when one dies that it creates fear. Here is what happens. The person you love slips out of their physical body and continues their existence on the astral plane. The astral plane is a lot like the physical world except the vibratory rate is different so the two of you can't physically connect in the same way. But they are alive well and happy in the astral plane. When they are on the astral plane, it is as real to them as the physical plane once was.

When they slip out of the body, they are usually greeted by loved ones who have already crossed, by their spirit guides or by angels. It is a wonderful experience to be welcomed to the other side. Immediately the person is caught up in the happiness of their new life on the astral plane and the only thing that really distracts them from that is the anguish of people they have left on earth.

Earth has a coarse vibratory rate compared to the astral plane, so people who are hurting emotionally on earth gain much stamina by pulling themselves out of it. That is the experience of the physical life. People on the astral plane can now see that and have great compassion for their loved ones left behind. They want to use any means to comfort you by sending you a sign somehow that you are misguided because they are fine and you are still connected by love. Someone may say something that was their catch phrase. Or, you may hear a song on the radio that depicts their connection with you. And the more that you look for these signs, the more they will be there.

When someone is crossing over, know that this is a wonderful time for them. Reminisce about all that you have experienced together and be grateful for the love. Let them pass on in peace and understanding that you will not pull on them when they are on the other side. The love is the commonality in your vibratory rates so that you can connect through subtle means regardless of where you are residing. Connect through the love; it is the only viable means anyway.

A technique when one has crossed over is to imagine that they are merely off on an errand or in another room. Because they are.

172 REAL TIME ASSISTANCE WITH PSYCHIC INFLUENCES

Hi Jen,

Please can you kindly suggest some taps that I can do in order to get entities that are attached to my body off? Please can you also suggest taps that I can do to get back my energy from the black adepts [witches, wizards]?

Yes.

Say each statement three times while tapping on your head and say it a fourth time while tapping on your chest.

"I remove all curses that have been put on me; in all moments."

"I send all energy matrices that are attached to me into the Light and Sound; in all moments."

"I command all complex energy matrices that are attached to me to be escorted into the Light and Sound by my guides; in all moments."

"I blow all energies that are trying to influence me out of my energy field and cause them to recoil from the force of my love; in all moments."

"I repair and fortify the Wei Chi of all my bodies; in all moments."

"I seal and heal all 32 layers of my auric field with the purity of Divine Love; in all moments."

"I am impervious to the influences of all unworthy intentions; in all moments."

"I am centered, empowered and protected in the sanctity of Divine Love; in all moments."

"I refuse access to all unworthy intentions; in all moments."

"I wither away all tentacles that use fear to breach the integrity of my beingness; in all moments."

"I am impervious to all attacks; in all moments."

There you go. These will do the trick.

173 ONLINE DATING SCAMMERS

The way society has progressed, people looking for a love interest are almost forced to search online dating sites to meet someone. It is the most convenient means of finding someone without stepping out of one's comfort zone.

Online dating sites are a useful tool and many have found a long term relationship from visiting them. But there is a vulnerability associated with subscribing to them. If people felt comfortable "putting themselves out there," they would most likely have the skills necessary to meet someone through more traditional means. But if someone hasn't met a mate in school or work, they may have to rely on someone to fix them up or just pray that fate has someone in mind for them.

Online dating is a necessary tool for many. The sad thing is that there are always opportunists ready to exploit the need or vulnerability of others. And the thing that makes online dating agreeable is the same thing that leaves one vulnerable. It's done with no one to oversee your safety or to be your better judgment. There is no one to tell you that what is too good to be true usually is.

Before getting vested in an illusion that some scammer has put out there to bait you with, here are some red flags. There may even be a formula of things to look out for when looking for a potential partner. These are things that could well be overlooked if you aren't savvy and really ready to meet someone. Let me save you some heartache.

First of all, be cautious in meeting someone on free sites or on the sites when they have free weekends. With no screening process, anybody can set up an account. You must be savvy and screen everyone yourself. In this one area, I would advise that you NOT rely solely on your good instincts. When it comes to love, we believe in what we want to believe and our good instincts may get overtaken by our hopes and desires.

It is best to be skeptical at first. If anyone you connect with challenges your caution, then that is the first red flag. Don't trust that the image you are seeing is actually that person. (We won't even address the fact that it could be them 20 years ago and they are in denial that they still don't look that way.)

Ask someone you meet to email you a photo of them with something relevant to validate their authenticity. Have them hold up a newspaper with the current date on it. Turn it into something of a fun task. If they are real, they may not feel comfortable but will understand why and comply.

Be cautious of someone who doesn't list criteria of their ideal date. If they say they are looking for inner beauty or inner connectedness, see that as a red flag. It may be true, but it is also the perfect thing for a scammer to say to prey on people who don't feel comfortable about themselves. Usually real people have something that they are attracted to and want to list that.

Be cautious of someone who is able to write very articulate love letters and say that they felt this instant connection with you. They may also say that they have been alone a long time, have not been on the market for some reason or another and are only looking for that one person. There may be an inconsistency in how often they write. They may write these letters that can make you melt, but they may not write every day and may talk of being very busy with their job and you are the only thing keeping them going.

The letters they write may be like a love sparring session where each one draws you in more and more. They will talk about how you have opened them up to love. Be cautious if someone says that they have had dreams about you and that you are their soul mate. They may start making long-term commitment plans about being with you without ever asking you the everyday questions that common sense would ask.

They may send you a questionnaire to get to know you better. It may ask your full name, address, and other personal information sandwiched in between ethereal questions about whether you like walks on the beach or not. Please don't give them your personal information. Be vague, skeptical or even deceptive at this point.

They won't seem interested in speeding things up; they seem content to continue this way. They may communicate by instant messaging, but may have many spelling errors. When this happens, look for an inconsistency in level of interest. They may have a different interest level on instant messaging. That is because you may have been handed over to someone else who is not as cunning in the deception.

Once they have established a long-term commitment with you and you have returned the sentiment, there will be a turn of events. Something dreadful will happen in their life where they need income from you and there is no other means of getting it. The story will be creative and they will be really convincing. They have no other means of assistance even though they tell you they are very rich.

They will tell you they need a certain amount of money but please send what you can. For some reason, they won't be able to accept the money and will ask you to send it to a third party. If you tell them you don't have it, their tone will change. They will challenge your loyalty and your authenticity with them. Please don't feel bad. This is what they do. I would not offend a harmless bottom feeder by comparing them to such low-lifes.

I believe that this whole scenario plays out more than people would ever admit to. I think that it happens to people and they are too ashamed and embarrassed to admit it. That is how evil lives--when no one speaks out against it. When you start to see some of the red flags listed above, move on. The more time you spend engaged in indulging such unethical behavior, the less time you will be devoting to finding a real mate: a real, flawed, partner with some baggage but also some redeeming qualities.

Please remember the (paraphrased) adage: if it is too good to be true, then it might still be true but just not here in this reality.

174 UNDOING NEGATIVE POSTS

Many people still believe it is helpful to post negative images on their page as a means of creating a reaction. Creating a reaction is not the same as benefiting a cause. Animals are in the moment and very sensitive to thoughts. So if you post a picture of an animal being abused, that animal is stuck in the abuse by everyone who sees him that way.

If you use an image to make people feel bad, then you are lowering their vibration to one of the same level as the picture. It is having a negative impact rather than a positive one. It used to be that one photo was so shocking that it would cause a reaction because it struck the psyche as wrong. But now, there are so many of them that people just get used to seeing them and become more complacent to the assault. There has got to be a better way.

Last night, someone posted an image of a dog's mouth and front and back paws all tied up with duct tape. You can't un-see that. I am certain the dog is not in that position now, but everyone who sees him is experiencing that horrific act and on some level, he is still trapped in the abuse. I spent much of the night in contemplation cutting off the duct tape and loving the puppy and all abused pets. It was my way of countering the abuse and negating the negative affects of the photo.

May I suggest that if you have a cause that you are passionate about, use your loving intention to saturate all the innocents with such kindness that it satiates them to the core. This is a beneficial way to support a cause without having your efforts be used to perpetuate the problem. No one wants to send money to drug lords. So make sure all of your efforts are used only to uplift. Send your love to every homeless puppy, abused child or faceless victim. It has the side affect of stretching your capacity to love and understanding your own capabilities.

175 WHO WE ARE

Who we are is an incredible mystery to unravel. See the totality of You.

Technique: Take inventory of the things that you are afraid of, the things that you naturally excel at, the time periods that you gravitate to in the movies, and the places you want to travel to or avoid. All are keys to who you have been and what you have experienced in past lives.

Some people avoid the concept of past lives because the trauma that they have endured is too close to the surface and they prefer to keep it buried. But if people can look at who they have been, they can make some adjustments in who they are now and save themselves a lot of unnecessary dis-ease.

For example, someone who has nightmares or is depressed, may be able to uncover the underlying cause of such things and face the intensity of them in the Light of the present existence.

176 DON'T BE A "HAS BEEN"

In my private sessions, at the end of the hour the client sometimes feels better than they may have felt in many lifetimes. The frustrating side effect of this is that the first thing out of their mouth is usually, "This is wonderful! I have been...." It is habit and they don't realize what they are doing, but they are unconsciously pulling back all that we just cleared with the words, "I have been."

Many of you have been interrupted by me in our exchanges. It may have registered as rude, but that was not my intention. I never listen to anyone tell me what they have been because they are bringing all their problems, all their dis-ease, and a lot of stagnant energy into the sacred moment of now. A couple of you do this in messaging me. I am writing and sending out good vibes and will be interrupted with no advance warning to, "I have been...." It is just poured right into my moment as subtle as if a landfill truck just backed up to my lap and poured its content. (If you are feeling bad right now, it wasn't you).

When I am with someone, it is a sacred exchange for me. I have been helping so many people release that it seems it happens spontaneously when others connect with me. Why would I allow anyone to contaminate a sacred altar with their problems. Why do you?

Think about the words that we use. The word "I" is a declaration of the divine. You are declaring yourself conscious and present in the moment. The word "have" is a word of abundance. It is linking the whole of the abundance with the declaration of you as the divine. The next word is very important. It defines the perimeters of the abundance. "I have Joy," "I have Abundance," "I have Freedom."

But the next word many people use taints the words, "I have…." It is the word "been." The word "been" is tugboat pulling all the struggle and pain that we have conquered and overcome to get to this glorious moment of now and dumps it right onto the altar of the present. "Been" has just desecrated the moment. It is a throw net collecting all our experiences and dragging them along into whatever joy that could ever be had. People wonder why they can't be happy and they don't understand when I tell them to let go of the net.

Think about the many times people use this word. Is it usually ever good when they say, "I have been"? You know how you can tell if this is something that you do, maybe unconsciously? If you are arguing in your mind about this statement, most likely you are someone who does this. Or, you may be someone who allows this to be done to you. Think about a time when you were having a great day and someone connects with you and starts with the "have been" and the joy of the moment wanes. They have just tainted your sacred moment.

Do yourself and those around you a favor. When they start to tell you how they have been, cut them off and ask them, "How are you right now?" Try to bring them into an understanding of now. Either they will get an understanding of it or leave you alone in the future because they didn't get what they wanted out the exchange. This is a small price for you to pay to honor the "I" within you.

177 YOU KNOW THAT FEELING OF JUST NEEDING TO COMPLAIN?

You know that feeling of just needing to complain? There is energy that is pressing inside so it needs to get expressed? Instead of giving it to someone who it may affect in a negative way, tell it to a tree. A tree doesn't feel burdened by it. A tree accepts all.

Bury all complaints into the ground so they can be used as soil to grow something beautiful and useful.

178 BE LIGHT AS A FEATHER

Problems are like feathers. One or two are light enough and we think nothing of holding them for others. But when they start to pile on, they can get heavier and heavier. It is best if we are going to listen to them, to let them blow away right afterwards.

But when we think about them, or worse, discuss them with others or dwell on them, it is like syrup that causes them to stick to us. Some people walk around carrying a whole pie of feathers and if you try to tell them, they will think that you are being ridiculous because one feather is so light.

It gets to the point that people can tell the feather carriers and know where to take all their extra feathers. The kinder thing to do is for everyone to send their problems in the wind and release them to dissolve into Love and Light.

179 ALLOW YOUR ATOMS TO DANCE!

Words like abuse, hate, broke, cancer and cursing have a very low vibratory rate. Words like Joy, Love, Abundance, Freedom and Happiness have a high vibratory rate. Every thing we say determines whether our atoms sink or dance. We choose.

We have all experienced traumas. That is the way we learn to thrive. We learn to thrive by outlasting and "out-loving" abuse. Some people need to release the energy of these experiences by venting. It is a step in the process. But when the venting becomes habitual and it is difficult to be around them, it is time to suggest professional help and step away. They are in a mind loop that all the sympathy in the world will not mend.

To continue to be around secondhand abuse (abuse that has happened to others but they keep referencing in conversation), is a form of self-abuse. One needs to take care of their own needs first so that they can stay centered in the love. Staying centered is the way to access infinite Joy and Love. It is vital to stay centered. Protect your center at all costs. Be an advocate for you.

180 BABIES

Babies are so beautiful because they are full of pure potential. Every time we are hurt or feel like we have failed, we shut that potential down. To me, that is what aging and dis-ease are about--shutting ourselves off to the flow of that potential energy.

Technique:

Say this statement three times while tapping the top of your head. Then say it a fourth time while tapping the center of your chest.

"I pour potential energy into every cell of my beingness and fill myself with Optimism, Joy, and Abundance; in all moments."

It may have a side effect of taking away your appetite because it really isn't food that you are craving.

181 ALTERNATIVE TO COUNTING SHEEP

To help you sleep, instead of counting sheep, tend to animals that are love starved.

Visualize yourself in a place where a starved animal is huddled. It could be a shelter or a cold alley or a deserted lot. Spoon him or her and pour your love into them. Wrap yourself around them. Melt away the pain and loneliness. This may be a natural way to fall asleep. It may even illicit dreams of helping more animals. Your love will actually be helping them.

182 SMILING WITH YOUR ENERGY

Before I knew I was a dynamic and gifted energy worker, I did not know my purpose. What I realize now is that my purpose was to merely stay alive and thrive with as much composure and kindness as possible. The Universe was showing me the worst in life so I could learn how to bring out the best. It is a form of alchemy to be able to spin gold out of anything we are given.

There are some out there still wondering what their purpose is. For some, it is merely to stay alive. The Universe will take every single crutch from you so that you realize how to rely solely on your own wits and your own connection to source. It is a beautiful lesson in empowerment to do so.

From my earliest memories, I was known for smiling. It was my way to connect to the world in love and claim a place for positivity in the world. The Universe will always teach us. At one of my lowest points, when I had only my smile to use as a tool to keep myself connected to love, the Universe took that away as well.

My face became totally paralyzed on one side. My face was frozen in one position. This lasted for years and it is still evident in my pictures. That is why I don't smile more. When I was looking out through my face, I was greeting everyone with warm kindness, but they were only seeing this expressionless gaze at them. I tried to smile with my eyes but they were affected too.

It was a very isolating time. I still loved people and I still wanted to connect. So I learned to smile with my energy. It is a form of smiling inside even though there is no outer evidence of it. It was a way for me to amp up my own energy system and enhance my own wattage. It was apparently a necessary lesson and I learned to observe life even more. Now, sometimes I can see my own inner light emanating from my body like heat on pavement.

The point is, if you don't know what your purpose is, then your purpose is to do whatever you are doing with love, grace and a grateful heart. Our lessons are custom made for us and no one can really appreciate what we have and still endure. It is not their job to know. Our job is to give our gifts in a way that makes it seem effortless, no matter how insignificant they may seem at the time. This is grace and this is how we smile with our energy.

If you want to empower yourself, smile with your energy in everything you do. Doing so is the "It Factor" of a persona. One has a choice. Either they can suck attention from others with their problems and requests for attention, or they can tap into perpetual love and give it out, unwavering under all circumstances. Either one can define you and it is a choice. But which one leads you to uncovering your greatness and connects you to perpetual love?

I guarantee that smiling in your energy will empower you more than any outer demand for attention can. When you smile inwardly, angels take notice. It is then that you tap into the same light that they emanate. You are turning on the luminescence of your true self.

183 WHY THE LAW OF ATTRACTION MAY NOT BE WORKING FOR YOU

The Law of Attraction is popular now. Many people recognize it and work with it effectively. The Law of Attraction states that you attract everything to your Universe by your thoughts. But those who try it and don't have results believe it is because of a flaw in the law itself.

There are many spiritual laws that are as exacting as gravity. If one is not working when you apply it, it's because you are inadvertently applying another law as well. Saying the Law of Attraction doesn't work for you is like believing that gravity only works sometimes. The laws that run the Universe are exacting.

If the Law of Attraction isn't working for you, maybe it is because you are trying to use it in a vacuum. For example, if you are trying to attract more love in your life but have negative feelings in some areas, maybe you are inadvertently applying the Law of Vibrations.

The Law of Vibrations says that everything resonates. What you think, say or do, and how you live determine the rate of vibration. Negative thoughts are more dense than optimistic thoughts. It matters little if the thoughts are about yourself or others.

Imagine people as tennis balls dropped onto the table. Tennis balls that are lighter will be able to bounce higher and will bounce in rhythm with other light balls. From eye level, the light balls see other light balls and not the more dense ones. Using this analogy, realize that people who apply positive energy to all aspects of their life are at eye level with other people that approach life similarly. This is the way we apply labels. In high school, we become the geek, nerds, jocks, etc. In life, we divide ourselves socially, economically and politically.

There is another spiritual law that comes into play that is relevant to the Law of Attraction. It is called the Law of Reversed Efforts. It simply means that the more attention is focused on a situation, the more it will elude the object of its attention. This is why two positive sides of a magnet repulse each other. The Law of Reversed Efforts is also what most daters have experienced when they have someone really interested in them, but when they show interest in return, the attraction fizzles.

The one spiritual law that is highly overlooked is the Law of Opposites. It just states that for every thought or action, there is an equal and opposing thought or reaction. This is why there is so much turmoil in the world. The belief that is prevalent now is that we need to take a stand or we are part of the problem. I believe that by creating a force in any one area, as noble as it is, creates an opposing force.

As with the other laws, it cannot be applied in a vacuum or else it becomes a weakness. But if one were to apply all of the laws in conjunction, it will uplift them and humanity in unforeseen ways. It only takes one side to diffuse an argument. And there is a huge difference between walking away from a fight and getting beat up. One is passive and the other is an empowering choice.

When applying the Law of Attraction, or even promoting your favorite cause, be certain to take into consideration the Law of Reversed Effort and the Law of Opposites. It's a way to lift yourself out of the emotional stranglehold you may be feeling and give you a vantage point where you can be much more effective. And when you are in a higher vantage point, you will be working with the Law of Detachment and also working with the most important Spiritual Law there is, the Law of Love.

184 ACTUALIZING SELF-LOVE

It seems like many of us are a living oxymoron. We spend so much of the human experience searching for true love and at the same time we expend so much thought energy diminishing ourselves and sabotaging our success.

False modesty and humility, it seems, have been so ingrained in our DNA that it takes a lot to override the compulsion to think ill of ourselves. We believe that to be humble we have to diminish ourselves. But humility should be gained from a point of strength rather than of weakness.

Instead of lowering the bar and seeing yourself as worthless, why not see yourself as dynamic and also see that potential in everyone else. That is a definition of humility that actually has a positive purpose.

All the people who are looking for love may do better to look in the one place that is so difficult to focus on. Why not discover love from within? It may sound cliché, but there really is a well of joy, contentment and sense of fulfillment by realizing one's own innate potential and making a habit of manifesting it. It may just be the missing link in finding the love of one's life.

It doesn't feel comfortable to set out to discover self-love so here is a little humorous technique to try.

When you are alone, think of all the love songs that you have ever heard. Sing them to yourself with one minor tweak. Whenever the word "you" comes up in the song, exchange it for "me." It sounds like a silly game but your brain works by programming. This is a gentle way to profess love for yourself and manifest it without doing much more than just playing this little song game.

The more cheesy it seems to do this, the more effective it could be to change deep programming within yourself. To get you started in the game, here are a list of some of the top wedding songs with a little twist. Sing these to yourself and make up a lot of your own, and when you have discovered the benefits of doing this, teach the game to your children and others who need to learn the lesson of self-love. Or, just share this article with them.

Love Songs:

"Everything I Do, I Do It For [Me]"	Bryan Adams
"Tonight I Celebrate My Love For [Me]"	Peabo Bryson & Roberta Flach
"[I] Light Up My Life"	Debby Boone
"I Got [Me] Babe"	Sonny and Cher
"[I Am] the Wind Beneath My Wings"	Bette Midler
"Hopelessly Devoted To [Me]"	Olivia Newton John
"Can't Smile Without [Me]"	Barry Manilow
"I Will Always Love [Me]"	Whitney Houston
"I Just Called To Say I Love [Me]"	Stevie Wonder

Maybe this game will jump start other ways to treat yourself with more respect. Maybe you will cut yourself off when you start to say something derogatory about yourself. Maybe you will stop giving silent agreement for people to make jokes about you.

Maybe this could start a snowball of self-love for you. You may start passing on the extra sweets, start eating healthier and taking healthy walks. You can get yourself out of unhealthy relationships and refuse to compromise in so many ways. You could move towards the dynamic you that we both know you are! And it could all start with a song!

185 CHOOSING LOVE

What if you had someone out there who was the love of your life many times. The mere thought of them brought you such joy, and being separated made you wilt with sadness.

What if they came to you beyond time and space and said, "I can't be your lover in this life, but I want to be near you, as close as possible. I want to feel your body in a totally different way. I want to feel totally protected and safe in your arms and to be free to express who I am more completely than I ever have. Will you help me? Will you make room for me in your life? Can you love me in a different way? I may not be in a perfect body. I have lessons to learn. You said at one point that you would do anything you could for me. Would you do this for me? Would you be my parent?"

What if your love came to you in a dream and said, "It is too stressful to be human, but I so desperately want to be with you. If I come to you in a different form, will you take care of me? It may be stressful to find you so I may develop bad habits. But once I feel the security of your home, I will do my best to please you. We may not be able to understand each other at first, but we will remember how good it is to be together. Will you rescue me from a shelter? In return, I will love you with my whole being. Will you even recognize me if I come to you in an animal body?"

Is there someone out there waiting to be loved by you? Is there someone already in your life that you have forgotten who they really are and how special your relationship is?

The mundane process of daily living sometimes causes us to shut down on all the possibilities. Remember how exciting it was when we were children and there was a new adventure around every corner? The adventures are still there, but they take a more subjective form. The truth is that we have all lived and loved beyond this world. The key is to remember the love and to remember who we are as eternal beings, that we are ambassadors of love.

There are always ways to bring new adventures into our life. It is by stretching our capacity to love. No one ever expands their world by playing it safe and shutting down the possibilities. The love that is right around the corner may be the love that you have been waiting for your whole life. If you suspend the restrictions you put on love, then you yourself will not be limited by those restrictions.

It is your choice. As with anything else, it is always your choice.

186 PROBLEM SOLVING TECHNIQUE

In contemplation, go back to every scenario where you were freaking out and show the old you how it worked out. Then think of what is going on now in the present. Wait for that same visit from the you in the future to tell you what to do to work things out.

187 TECHNIQUE TO CUT THE DRAMA

When we are in an argument or are violated, we want validation about our response. Did we overreact? Or we want reassurance that we are not being judged too harshly for our actions. So we talk about the event and encourage others to pacify us. It is a tedious, energy zapping process that is a hit and miss whether we will get the desired results.

By asking others about a private incident, we are inviting them in. They may have a reaction to the explosive energy that has been stirred up and may end up attacking as a form of protection. There is a better way.

Sit in contemplation and inwardly see yourself as the center of the Universe where all the stars and planets are moving around you...or are supposed to. See all the strings that are between you and the planets and other heavenly bodies. With your intention, cut the strings. That is it. Simply cut all the strings that you sense between yourself and everything that should be rotating in your orbit. You are the center of your Universe. You can and are meant to be free and untethered.

As you cut the strings, watch the planets and all matter pull away and start to orbit naturally around you. Continue doing this until all the strings are cut and you are centered in this incredible, peaceful center with everything naturally flowing around you in perfect order. If you see any strings dangling, dissolve them with your mind.

This is how to address any issue. This is addressing it at the core. There is no need to come out of your center even more than the issue has already caused. Using this technique can become so habitual that you will be able to go the center as an issue is happening and cut the strings immediately. Every experience is an opportunity to strengthen our own ability to maintain our own balance. Instead of having an aversion to them, we can see them as opportunities for spiritual growth.

188 STOP BEING A KNOW IT ALL

(Say each statement three times while tapping on your head and say it a fourth time while tapping on your chest.)

"I release being a 'know it all'; in all moments."

"I release sabotaging my spiritual growth by being a 'know it all'; in all moments."

"I shift my paradigm from a 'know it all' to the 'awakened in all'; in all moments."

189 BEING AGREEABLE

I facilitated a session recently with a client who is very agreeable. But in her voice was an irritating quality that was off-putting. One of her issues was that other people got irritated with her and she didn't understand why. She went out of her way to be nice.

During her session, I presented a deep understanding about herself to her. She accepted this truth as if she already knew it, which she did not. It was a clue into the dynamics that play out in her everyday life.

In this life, her father is a lawyer. She learned early that she was not going to win an argument with him. Her way of coping was to agree. Saying yes was a way to placate others and to keep them from inundating her.

Here are some taps that may help someone who uses "yes" too much:

(Say each statement three times while tapping your head and a fourth time while tapping your chest.)

"I release using 'yes' as a fortress; in all moments."

"I release the fear of saying 'no'; in all moments."

"I release confusing speaking my truth with creating chaos; in all moments."

"I release associating chaos with death; in all moments."

"I release sacrificing my truth to placate others; in all moments."

"I release the trauma of being tortured for my truth; in all moments."

190 TECHNIQUE TO RIGHT PAST TRANSGRESSIONS

You know all those interactions and scenarios that bring anxiety when thinking about them? Remember the times when you were wronged, rejected or diminished in some way, or the times you weren't as kind or loving as you could have been and hurt someone? They cause a heaviness that is difficult to carry around.

During a quiet time, comb over all the experiences that have caused anguish. Visualize taking snapshot of them. As you take a snapshot of each one, take the photo and toss it in a pile. Take as many photos as you need in as many different scenarios as possible. Make a big pile.

When all the scenarios are exhausted and there is a huge pile of photos, visualize taking a spark of Divine Love and setting the pile in a blaze. Know that divine love is burning out all the energy of the experiences. Visualize the fumes going back to whatever person was wronged and giving them back what the experience took from them. Don't focus on any one individually. Just know that everyone is coming to balance as the experiences are cleansed out of your causal memory banks.

After the whole pile has burned and cooled, see that all that is left is a pile of ash. See a breeze blow in and sweep away the ashes to reveal little nuggets of gold. See that nothing is left but the beautiful little nuggets. Visualize picking up each little piece of gold and placing them against your heart. Have them melt into your heart. Feel them dissolve from your hand and absorb deep into your body through your heart. Feel uplifted by the process. Be energized by the awareness that you have righted deep wrongs. Feel the happiness and freedom.

191 CONFUSING ANGER FOR STRENGTH

I recently had a private session with a woman who was drawn to angry people. As much as she abhorred the behavior, there was something about the anger that she was drawn to. During her session, Santa Claus came through. From that image, I realized that she was confusing anger for strength, authority and completeness. She felt weak because she didn't indulge in anger.

Her past life in a puritanical religion revealed itself during her session. She saw God as an angry God. In this lifetime, devoting herself to knowing God, she got the wires mixed up through past programming that God was angry. Since she outgrew anger in herself long ago, the only way she felt she could get closer to God was by having relationships with angry people.

We untangled the misconceptions that were preventing her from having a personal relationship with Joy, Love, Abundance, Freedom and Wholeness, which are all attributes of God.

Here are some of the taps that we used. They may help you, as well.

(Say each statement three times while tapping the head and say it a fourth time while tapping the chest.)

"I release confusing anger for strength; in all moments."

"I release the belief that I am weak; in all moments."

"I release the fear of anger; in all moments."

"I release revering anger; in all moments."

"I release the belief that God is angry; in all moments."

"I release using angry people to compensate; in all moments."

"I release confusing anger for Love; in all moments."

192 TECHNIQUE FOR SOMEONE WHO CONFRONTS YOU

When someone is annoyed at you and confronts you for something that they are passionate about, the primal response is to be defensive. Being defensive is a primal urge. It is important to learn to advance beyond primal urges and knee-jerk reactions. It is also important to learn to stay in your center and not retreat out of need to be polite or fear of confrontation.

When someone is annoyed with you, search your memory banks for when you were annoyed in a similar way. That is meeting them on equal ground. Don't say you understand until you have done this. If you do, that is patronizing and very offensive. It comes off arrogant and condescending. People are savvy enough to know the difference.

Once you do understand the stance of the other party, explain in a clear and concise way how you went from that point of view that you were at to your present one. Take them on a quick journey with you, so they can now meet you at the point you are at. It is that simple. What you are really doing is folding time and space between the two of you so you can be in agreement if you choose to be.

It is a wonderful exercise in compassion and self-empowerment. Please try it, and feel how it can shift any disagreement into being on common ground.

193 TECHNIQUE FOR DISARMING ANGER

Here is a very healing and liberating technique:

Take all the anger that someone has built up for a very long time. They are now targeting it at you. Take it. Let them pour it into the Universe through you as your individual self backs out of the way and allows it passage. Let them just empty their whole load. Just take it.

You may feel yourself tremble as the magnitude passes through, but don't allow it to hook into your emotions or thoughts. See it as a passing deluge of energy that has nothing to do with you except that you are a portal into the Universe for it to release. Be that detached about it. Just let it all dump out.

This is a way to dismantle it because anger is a reserve that needs to be tapped and released. When two people are angry, they are merely bouncing the same energy back to each other and adding more as they go. It is a game. The winner is the one who can leave unscathed. So when you let the energy pass through you, it is no different than refusing to throw a basketball back to someone who has just sent it to you.

Refuse to give the anger back. They will try to goad you into doing that but simply take their anger from them and don't give it back. It is as simple as that. It is the same as taking the ball out of any game. Without the ball, there is no game. Can you imagine the peace that will reside when everyone understands this simple technique and practices it?

Anger is energy. The sender may have a lot of it built up. But once they empty their bank account of it, it is gone. The problem is with many angry people they keep getting dividends on their return. Don't give them any. They will become anger bankrupt in no time. The key is to be so very detached that you welcome their anger as a means of getting it out of the environment and preventing everyone else and the world from being poisoned by it.

Think of anger as a toxic gas and you are the hazmat operator who is merely extracting it from the world with your professionalism, non-reaction and new found vantage point. You may now welcome the anger as a solution to ridding the world of it.

A very beneficial side benefit of this is that you will no longer care if you make people angry. Once you practice passing the anger through, you are free. You can say and do whatever you need to say and do to be your most authentic self.

194 BECOME A TOXIC-FREE ZONE

People try to pull us into their drama. They try to get us to debate them or entice us with gossip. They try to pull us down to their level by piquing our curiosity, stroking our ego or stirring an emotional response.

If we don't respond, they get their feelings hurt. They may accuse us of cutting them off or acting superior. They may even accuse us of judging them. These are unconscious, manipulative techniques to keep us engaged with them.

Here are some responses to have handy to get yourself free:

"I really don't want to listen to others' problems. I have enough on my plate with my own issues."

"I care about you, but you are not your problems. Let me hear about you."

"I don't watch the news. Not interested."

"I don't engage in current events. It is a waste of energy."

"I don't talk about others. I don't want them talking about me."

"What you are talking about makes me feel wilted. I will have to disengage soon."

"Tell me good things."

You can ignore all the negative statements and when they say something positive, reward them with being engaged.

I use the following for shock value. I tell people "I don't care". What I mean is that I don't want to be in agreement with their problems. It takes them aback and it breaks through that unconscious habit of dumping. Of course I care, but I don't care to be dumped on. There is a huge difference.

195 PUTTING PERSONAL ASSAULTS INTO PERSPECTIVE

Think of a battle ground. Everyone is in a fight for their life and knows that everyone else is in the same situation. If they bump into someone else, it is just assumed that it is an accident and just part of the situation. They aren't walking around saying excuse me to others. They are too involved in fending off the next assault. Maybe this is a way to put personal assaults into perspective.

People aren't walking around trying to hurt others or worrying about making amends. People are caught up in the battle of life. Most people are grappling with what they are dealing with and it may never occur to them to look around at what they have caused.

196 NEGATE NEGATIVITY

We manifest our reality with our thoughts. When people have trouble relying on their own thoughts, they defer to the opinions of their friends. A true friend will assist someone to manifest the most profound reality possible. When a seemingly true friend tells you things that are limiting or hurtful in the name of being honest, they are not friends. They are indulging in power trips at your expense.

Anyone who says, "I don't want you to get hurt," is saying something hurtful. They will diminish your possibilities if you allow them to. Walk away and never look back. That is not a true friend but someone who is jealous and petty.

Friends don't squelch friends' dreams, hopes, aspirations or self-image. There are people to whom this is happening now. Please keep empowering yourself and negate the naysayers. They are secretly envious of you. It is, in a way, a compliment. Try to see it that way.

197 EMPOWERED IN FRIENDSHIP

Let's put things in perspective. The driver who cuts us off in traffic, the person who makes an offhand comment, the co-worker who teases us or the person with different opinions from ours are not enemies. An enemy is our antithesis that is so driven by the primal fear of being destroyed that they will do anything for self-preservation. They are driven to unmentionable acts out of self-preservation.

In peace, there are no enemies. There is just a haunting memory of the primal urge to survive at all costs during hostile times. These memories reveal themselves at the most inopportune time. They prod us when we are feeling the most vulnerable, when we are the most at peace, or when we merely want to love and be loved.

If we could get an overview of any battle, we would see how both sides use their foot soldiers as pawns for their thirst for power. Emotions, beliefs and fears would be manipulated to enhance the threat that the opposing side posed.

Here is a visualization: Imagine any battle in history. Look at it from a detached place of an overview. Make your love more expansive than a billions suns. Pour incredible love into every player on the battlefield. See them all being brought to complete bliss. See the love permeating the whole scene so both sides are filled with complete love. See the love satiate everyone and everything so there is no division. Visualize everything dissolve in the love.

Do these taps:

(Say each statement three times while tapping on your head and say it a fourth time while tapping on your chest.)

"I forgive all offenses; in all moments."

"I release harboring animosity for anyone or anything; in all moments."

"I release being a pawn for power plays; in all moments."

"I release making enemies; in all moments."

"I shift my paradigm from enemies to friends; in all moments."

"I am centered and empowered in friendship; in all moments."

198 TECHNIQUE TO STRETCH YOUR CAPACITY FOR COMPASSION

Having compassion is understanding what another person is going through by relating it to your own issues. As you go through your day, find common ground between yourself and every soul you meet. Get a sense of their journey by delving into a similar situation within yourself that allows you to understand their vantage point. No matter how radically different or how polar opposite someone is from you, whether they are a person, dog, or fish, there is still some way to relate.

When we find common ground to relate to someone, love can flow laterally. We are assisting the fluidity of love in the world. We are doing our part.

One reason the world has become so complacent is because of all the false limits imposed on people. They have clipped the wings of angels, dried up the dreams of dreamers, and left such a narrow bridge to success that almost no one makes it across.

What some call your "freak flag" is really your wings. The world needs every freak to continue to fly, every weirdo to continue to be weird, every dynamo to be dynamic, every inspirational speaker to continue to inspire.

It is through the unique, funny, strange, and different that those false limitations will fall away and we all will find freedom. Freedom is never found in the ordinary. That is where complacency dwells.

199 THE FRUIT OF YOUR OWN TREE

Instead of thinking of karma as a punishment, think of it as a delayed reaction. Instead of there being other souls in the world, there is only you. You look like you are in different form just to keep you on your toes. Everyone you interact with is you. That is it.

When you are mean to others, you are being mean to yourself with a delayed reaction on it. When you tease others you tease yourself. When you wish others harm you are wishing it for yourself. There is no point in stealing because you are just stealing from yourself. When looking at it this way, see if stealing still appeals to you.

When you pour incredible kindness and love into others, you are pouring it into yourself. Some already have a vague understanding of this, but the more everyone realizes this, the more all can enjoy the fruits of their own tree.

200 THE FROZEN TREE TECHNIQUE

Sometimes we are so frozen in our responses and our state of being that we are like a tree that has been coated with ice during a freezing rain storm. Ice is just rain that has frozen due to lack of warmth (love, acceptance). Instead of rolling off, it creates invisible layers that enshroud the tree. It is heavy and brittle and if the temperature doesn't change, the branches start to snap off; if it continues, the whole trunk collapses as well.

Visualize yourself as a tree that is covered in ice. Imagine the beautiful brilliant sun coming out and warming the climate. The cold ice pellets now become laced beauty that shroud you for an instant before they all melt into beautiful diamonds of crystal. Acknowledge your own beauty, even in this heavy state of endurance.

Now, feel the weight on you lighten as the water rolls off your trunk. Feel your branches return to a limber state. Feel how your branches reach up to the sky and how the warmth of the sun warms the sap inside you. Feel the sap run through your inner channels. Feel your roots secure you deep within the earth. Feel grounded, strong and supported by the vastness of the earth's depth.

Feel how strong and solid you really are. Everything that transpires is transitory compared to your vast existence planted deep in the earth and warmed by the brilliance of the sun. All life sings in your branches or dances at your base. Chaos may blow around you, but you stay nimble and grounded in the earth. You welcome experiences. See them as plentiful and natural as growing the leaves on every extension of your being.

Your experiences, like the leaves, serve a purpose for a season, but when you have learned the lesson, they all blow away. You do not hang on to them and cry because you lost a leaf. You rejoice because their departure signifies another cycle of growth, another ring of expansion defined in your core.

You are a wise tree, with deep roots like the oak and flexible branches like the willow. You are aromatic like the spruce and form a majestic silhouette on the horizon. Feel your strength. Feel your wisdom. Feel your endurance. Rejoice at the cycles of life. Feel the warmth of the sun sustain you and know all the experiences that you endure keep you interested in continuing to grow and expand and to be the majestic being that you are.

201 TECHNIQUE TO LISTEN

When you want to get a point across to someone, the means to do it is by listening to them. Listening creates a bridge of understanding and openness.

If you only want to exercise your concept of being right, then talk over them, put down things they say, and point out their flaws in thinking. What that does is activate their walls of protection. This protection is primal and so your most articulate point is going to be lost on everyone but you.

Communication isn't just about hearing the words. Communication is about receiving the other person like an invited guest into your inner sanctum.

202 TECHNIQUE TO BRING OTHERS TO THEIR SENSES

If people sit by, watch and allow a dictator to take over the leadership of this country then they deserve what they get. There are two choices being offered: fear, ignorance and powerlessness, or a mass awakening and choosing empowerment.

The passion and power that those immersed in fear and rhetoric are giving to one side should be accessed to take back empowerment from those who wish to enslave the whole world. Why aren't more people disturbed by this?

Are we watching the same current events? One man is bragging about how many people he will torture and never shows a hint of understanding how to operate affairs. The other man has been fighting his whole life for just causes and fair laws that help people.

It seems like everyone is watching the Book of Revelations play out. Those in ignorance who think that they are backing the positive choice are supporting evil. Torture, judging, control in the name of righteousness is all Satan's wheelhouse. Those who are tyrannical in their views on God and righteousness are being deceived by the devil.

The devil is creating a smokescreen for those who are sincere worshippers to make them believe they are righteous and holy. But they are being used to condone unholy things. Those of us who are not swayed by the influential hypnotism of the devil's pawn must do our part to pour more love, kindness and awareness into the world to dissipate this acrid cloud of illusion of fear and self-righteousness condoning the diminishing and belittling of others.

203 RAISE YOUR VIBRATION

We are all a frequency of sound like a certain channel on a radio station. If someone doesn't like you, it may merely be that they are a totally different frequency than you. You may be like a radio station to them that is not tuned to their frequency.

Someone can hurt you only if you resonate at a lower or equal frequency. If you are at a higher frequency, they may try to change your vibration by annoying you or trying to illicit sympathy from you. They may try to feed lower vibrations into your stream by talking about problems or illness. The worst is to do both--to talk about illness and to illicit sympathy.

The way not to be affected or hurt by anyone is to maintain the highest frequency possible. This entails staying focused on the positive. Love is the purest frequency. It doesn't matter what you love. It only matters that you stay loving and possible. It doesn't mean that you have to direct love to the person who is trying to affect you. It may be more helpful to stay detached from them.

It would be much more beneficial to attune to love any way possible and then direct it to the self.

204 GOODWILL

Jealousy, pettiness, one upping others are all ways to pinch one's energy. Kindness, generosity, encouragement, gregariousness, enthusiasm and wild abandonment create an expansive, fluid energy flow. A good way to manifest Joy, Love, Abundance, Freedom and Wholeness for yourself is to support those windfalls for everyone. You will wholeheartedly be swept up and carried along on the goodwill you offer to others.

205 CHOOSE TO IMPROVE

When you want to add any endeavor to your life, you need to create space for it. For example, if you want more clients, you may put together a directory where you store all the contact information. If a you want better health, create a part of your life and attention dedicated to health, etc.

It really doesn't matter what the initial process is. The important thing is to put more attention on your goal. It is just a matter of clearing out space for it somewhere. If you really are stuck, it may be all that you can do is to research something you are interested in online or to collect pictures. This is something.

Everything of a positive nature moves you towards a positive result. Every indulgent, self-defacing thought and comment digs you further into a rut. We all choose moment by moment. Why not choose to improve?

206 HOW TO STAY "IN LOVE"

When we fall in love, it is the most wonderful feeling. Love is the most divine form of energy. We are actually seeing our own divine nature using the other person as a mirror. When we want to give to our partner, it keeps us open to being a conduit for love. The trick to staying in love is staying in the desire to give. It keeps our own love energy flowing.

What stops the flow of energy is when we expect to receive from the other person. It is like flipping a switch from divine love to ego gratification. Whenever we give something to our mate and expect something in return, it is a subtle form of manipulation. We have taken the divine and debased it.

I have watched the formula of spiraling down between lovers many times. At first it's paradise, but then a nagging thought comes into the equation. Something as small as a slight misunderstanding. But the mind incessantly replays a tiny transgression and builds upon it. Before too long, there is a laundry list of reasons this person is totally wrong for you. The relationship seems hopeless.

Watching this process in yourself is a great way to learn how to overcome negative thoughts. The thoughts have their own agenda. They want to create drama for the ego so that the ego can feel alive. There are people out there who live in a constant state of upheaval. It gives them purpose. But if you don't need the drama and want to move beyond it, simply turn off the negative flow of thoughts as they come in.

Becoming aware of negative thoughts is an accomplishment in itself because they come in so subtly. Once recognized, they can automatically be dissipated by imagining them dissolving in the ethers. If it is difficult to do, create a visual technique. See the thoughts on a chalkboard and imagine erasing them, or pick the string of thoughts out of the air and drop them in a wastebasket. Editing thoughts helps with relationships, health issues, daily concerns and overall wellbeing.

Another way to keep your love divine is to realize that the main purpose that the other person fulfills is to be the recipient of your love. The gratitude will help keep the relationship in a positive light. If all the agreements this person honors with you are met with gratitude, then you're well on your way to understanding, experiencing and demonstrating divine love.

207 BREAKING UP GRACEFULLY

Isn't it interesting that when there is a breakup of a relationship, many times the individuals feel the need to demonize the other? Do you know why they do this? It serves a purpose.

When two people are together, they are mingling their energies and have relinquished all boundaries. When the relationship has run its course, the two try to separate, but their energies are so entwined that it is difficult. Hate consolidates energy and makes it very hard. Love expands energy and makes it very soft. When one is trying to get free of another, they use hate to separate their energy from the other. They use insults to kick off of the other's energy. Neither are necessary.

In contemplation, visualize an orb of energy that is really two orbs overlaying each other. In your mind, separate them gently from each other. Make certain that each is whole and complete and has everything that is an aspect of them. Completely separate them from each other. Make certain that each one is whole and has a great outer boundary. It is more than okay to leave them better than they were.

Think of two broken people as two broken orbs that filled in the other's fractured components. When separating the orbs, see that the connection taught them how to be whole. They no longer have to plug up their holes with the energy of someone else. When you visualize the separation of the two orbs, see them learning how to be whole from the other. See them both as vibrant, empowered self-contained orbs. Fortify any gaps or weak areas in both with the intention of pouring love into them and surrounding both with incredible love.

This is how we should leave each relationship that we enter. This is the way to heal through our interactions with others instead of fracturing each other. Use this same technique and go through all your past relationships. Do it not only with romantic partnerships, but with friends, family members and business relationships. In this way, you will be doing with each interaction what was spiritually intended for all: Gleaning from each other's gifts and becoming greater than you have ever been.

208 DIVORCE

I recently had a private session with someone who was starting the divorce procedures. They were gearing up and bracing for a battle. Energetically, that was exactly what they were doing. They were reliving going to war. It was not necessary.

We come together with such love and passion that we think that we have to remove our energies from each other with venom and hate. It is a process, it is true, to separate our energy field from the joint orb that we have melded it into. But it can be done with kindness if it is done with awareness.

In our private sessions, I helped this person separate their energies from their spouse by doing SFT taps where they remove all the vows and agreements between themselves and the spouse and take back their Joy. There is also a way to dissolve the marriage with such thoughtfulness that peace never has to be disturbed and love can prevail.

We are evolved enough to figure out the process of living and remaining totally in the love as well. That includes allowing everyone else to remain in the love.

If you are going through the process of divorce, you may want to try these taps. It doesn't have to be so hard.

(Say each statement three times while tapping on your head, and say it a fourth time while tapping on your chest.)

"I release confusing divorce with going to battle; in all moments."

"I release creating conflict to separate from my spouse; in all moments."

"I release using hate to separate from my spouse; in all moments."

"I release using conflict to justify my freedom; in all moments."

"I release creating drama to depart from the marriage; in all moments."

"I release hating my spouse; in all moments."

"I release defining divorce as the absence of love; in all moments."

"I release falling out of the love; in all moments."

"I am centered in love; in all moments."

209 STOP FEELING LIKE A FIFTH WHEEL

You know that uncomfortable feeling when two of your best friends are fighting and you are caught in the middle? You know that helpless feeling when one of your children is in a relationship with someone who doesn't seem to be good for them? Even if they do have a working relationship, it may still do something unpleasant to your insides to witness their dance. You know that person you have been watching on the sidelines just waiting for them to exhaust their present relationship?

Maybe it would be better if you didn't care so much. Maybe your involvement is keeping them bonded in some way. Maybe you would benefit the cause a lot more by being removed from the whole situation. I know you have tried. You don't have to do anything different outwardly. Just do this exercise.

(Say each statement three times out loud while tapping on the top of your head at the crown chakra and say it a fourth time while tapping on your chest at the heart chakra. Insert the first names of both parties in the relationship. Put the person you have your loyalty in the first line.)

"I release being the third wheel; in all moments."

"I release feeling dependent on _____ & _____'s dance; in all moments."

"I release feeling beholden to _____ & _____'s dance; in all moments."

"I release being enslaved to _____ & _____'s dance; in all moments."

"I recant all vows and agreements between myself and _____ & _____'s dance; in all moments."

"I remove all curses between myself and _____ & _____'s dance; in all moments."

"I remove all blessings between myself and_____ & _____ 's dance; in all moments."

"I sever all strings and cords between myself and _____ & _____ 's dance; in all moments."

"I dissolve all karmic ties between myself and _____ & _____ 's dance; in all moments."

"I remove all the pain, burden, limitations and engrams that _____ & _____ 's dance has put on me; in all moments."

"I remove all the pain, burden, limitations and engrams that I have put on _____ & _____ 's dance; in all moments."

"I take back all the Joy, Love, Abundance, Freedom, Health, Success, Security, Companionship, Creativity, Peace, Life, Wholeness, Beauty, Enthusiasm, Contentment, Spirituality, Enlightenment and Confidence, Intellect and the Ability to Discern that _____ & _____ 's dance has taken from me; in all moments."

"I give back all that I have taken from _____ & _____ 's dance; in all moments."

"I withdraw all my energy from _____ & _____ 's dance; in all moments."

"I release resonating with _____ & _____ 's dance; in all moments."

"I release emanating with _____ & _____ 's dance; in all moments."

"I remove all of _____ & _____ 's dance from my sound frequency; in all moments."

"I remove all of _____ & _____ 's dance from my light body; in all moments."

"I shift my paradigm from _____ & _____ 's dance to Joy, Love, Abundance, Freedom, Health, Success, Security, Companionship, Creativity, Peace, Life, Wholeness, Beauty, Enthusiasm, Contentment, Spirituality, Enlightenment, Confidence, Intellect and the Ability to Discern; in all moments."

"I strip all illusion off of _____ & _____ 's dance; in all moments."

"I transcend _____ & _____ 's dance; in all moments."

"I repair and fortify the Wei Chi on all my bodies; in all moments."

"I align all my bodies; in all moments."

"I am centered and empowered in divine love; in all moments."

"I make space in this world to know true love; in all moments."

"I remove all blockages to knowing true love; in all moments."

"I stretch my capacity to recognize true love; in all moments."

"I stretch my capacity to embrace true love; in all moments."

210 CHANGING FRIEND DYNAMICS

When someone is telling you about their problems, they will say things like, "You know how it feels when _____."

You are feeling just fine, but they want you to remember a time when you felt like they do so that you will be able to relate to their pain. They are actually pulling your vibratory rate down to their level so you are equals. In that similar frequency, problems can transfer easily between the two of you. They can relieve some of their angst by putting some of it on you. Since you are at similar levels then, it is like water passing between the two of you.

As payment for this, the person will flatter you shamelessly for being a good friend and a good listener. They go about their day feeling relieved and you may now feel out of sorts. But that is the price to pay for being a good friend. Right? Wrong.

This relationship dynamic has been going on for too long. Someone can be a great friend without listening to all that a person can dish out. Some people have become very crafty in getting their needs met this way. It is not fair to the friend.

How hard is it to say to someone that you are sorry they are feeling bad, you validate them and what they are going through, but you can't listen to all the venting? Suggest maybe that they go journal on everything that is bothering them and when they finish you can reconnect for a brainstorming session. This is a great way to honor all sides in the scenario.

The human psyche wasn't designed to process all the pain and problems of multiple people. The only way to stay present and healthy for all is to create and maintain healthy, loving and respectful boundaries. It can be done by always coming from love. This includes self-love!

211 BEING POPULAR

There are people who are very insightful, intelligent people, but for some reason, they aren't acknowledged or embraced very easily by others. They have a lot to offer and aren't readily accepted, so they overcompensate and develop the belief that the problem is a cosmetic one.

Personalities are our own unique signature on the world. It is a great way to size each other up. The problem is that some people try so hard to develop a personality that they don't realize that their true essence is already speaking to others.

We all have an energy field. We read each other's energy all the time. So if what is perceived in a person's energy field doesn't complement their personality, they are deemed as phony.

Here's an example: Someone is trying hard to fit in with the popular crowd so they try to wear the right shoes and know the right information even though their interests lie elsewhere. It's obvious to everyone except the person trying to be something they're not.

The reason why the cool kids are the cool kids is because their personality and energy systems align. It is a strength that is palpable. Then others want to copy the cool kids so they step out of who they really are to imitate them. Those are the people called hangers-on. We have all seen this.

Sometimes when you are overlooked and feel ignored, you may think it is because you are deficient in an area. It may be the opposite. You may have such strong energy that it is difficult to energetically look at you or be around you. And then if you try to overcompensate, energetically it is literally repulsive.

If you are feeling this aversion from others, maybe instead of adding things to your personality, try to be more subtle and see what happens. Have you ever been extraordinarily quiet and then have people shockingly concerned with what is wrong? They are feeling the centered-ness of you in that moment and responding.

It is very positive and uplifting to be able to step back and enjoy being your own self without the need for validation. It's a great self-discipline.

212 CRAVING OR AVOIDING ATTENTION

It was an unwritten rule growing up that I was not to receive compliments. There is a whole backstory behind the reasoning that isn't necessary to get into. It was just one of those agreements that I came into this life with and it gave me the perfect set of circumstances to hone my individual skill set.

Approval came in two forms: lack of negative attention and overhearing my mother brag about me to a third party. That was the way, as a child, that I received validation. It occurs to me that others may have developed an attraction or an aversion to attention through their experiences.

Here are some taps to assist:

(Say each statement three times while tapping on your head and say it a fourth time while tapping on your chest.)

"I release confusing attention with love; in all moments."

"I release craving attention; in all moments."

"I release defining all attention as negative; in all moments."

"I release the need to be invisible; in all moments."

"I release the need to avoid attention; in all moments."

"I release the fear of being called out; in all moments."

"I release being defined by others; in all moments."

"I release allowing attention to knock me out of my center; in all moments."

"I shift my paradigm from seeking attention to knowing love; in all moments."

213 RELATIONSHIP WORKSHEET

The biggest issue that people seem to lament about is getting over a relationship with another person. That is because when you are intimate with someone, you swap energy freely. But when you part, you have left an energetic aspect of yourself with them. You walk around talking about them because you are trying to get your essence back from them. Here is the protocol to do just that.

Now you never have to suffer at the hands of a past lover and be left un-whole. Now you don't have to be hesitant to give all of yourself to the next person because now you have the means to energetically regain your empowerment. In fact, because these taps are performed "in all moments" you are safeguarded from being fragmented in the future as well.

This protocol is simply meant to put your fate back in your own hands where it should be. It is not merely words. Doing this protocol is you being the shaman; it is you being empowered. It is you taking back your energy and releasing the things that have been weighing you down. It is also repairing your energy field so that you are not susceptible in the future. It is you taking back your empowerment and freeing you to love as unabashedly as you truly desire without the fear of being annihilated in the process.

It may feel so freeing to do these taps for past partners that you may want to do them regarding every person in your life. You may want to untangle yourself from every family member, co-worker, boss and friend. You may even want to do this protocol with every organization or idea that has held you back. Here is to you freeing yourself in a very profound way. Maybe in releasing all entanglements, you can finally get an understanding of who you really are unhindered and free.

You can make it a practice to do this once a day with a different person. You can even do it with groups, subjects, concepts, and anything else that limits your freedom.

(Say each statement three times out loud while tapping on the top of your head at the crown chakra and say it a fourth time while tapping on your chest at the heart chakra.)

"I release being with _____ out of habit; in all moments."

"I release feeling dependent on _____; in all moments."

"I release feeling beholden to _____; in all moments."

"I release being enslaved to _____; in all moments."

"I remove all vivaxes between myself and _____; in all moments."

"I remove all tentacles between myself and _____; in all moments."

"I remove the claws of _____ from my beingness; in all moments."

"I remove all programming and conditioning that _____ has put on me; in all moments."

"I remove all engrams of _____ from my beingness; in all moments."

"I send all energy matrices into the Light and Sound that limit my freedom in regards to _____; in all moments."

"I command all complex energy matrices that limit my freedom in regards to _____ to be escorted into the Light and Sound by my Guides; in all moments."

"I strip all illusion off of my dynamics with _____; in all moments."

"I withdraw all my energy from _____; in all moments."

"I eliminate the first cause in regards to _____; in all moments."

"I remove all masks, walls and armor that I have worn because of _____; in all moments."

"I nullify all contracts with _____; in all moments."

"I recant all vows and agreements between myself and _____; in all moments."

"I remove all curses between myself and _____; in all moments."

"I sever all strings and cords between myself and _____; in all moments."

"I dissolve all karmic ties between myself and _____; in all moments."

"I remove all the pain, burden, limitations and engrams that _____ has put on me; in all moments."

"I remove all the pain, burden, limitations and engrams that I have put on _____; in all moments."

"I take back all the Joy, Love, Abundance, Freedom, Health, Success, Security, Companionship, Creativity, Peace, Life, Wholeness, Beauty, Enthusiasm, Contentment, Spirituality, Enlightenment and Confidence that _____ has taken from me; in all moments."

"I give back all that I have taken from _____; in all moments."

"I release resonating with _____; in all moments."

"I release emanating with _____; in all moments."

"I remove all of _____ from my sound frequency; in all moments."

"I remove all of _____ from my light body; in all moments."

"I shift my paradigm from _____ to Joy, Love, Abundance, Freedom, Health, Success, Security, Companionship, Creativity, Peace, Life, Wholeness, Beauty,

Enthusiasm, Contentment, Spirituality, Enlightenment and Confidence; in all moments."

"I strip all illusion off of _____ for myself; in all moments."

"I transcend _____; in all moments."

"I repair and fortify the Wei Chi on all my bodies; in all moments."

"I align all my bodies; in all moments."

"I am centered and empowered in Joy, Love, Abundance, Freedom, Health, Success, Security, Companionship, Creativity, Peace, Life, Wholeness, Beauty, Enthusiasm, Contentment, Spirituality, Enlightenment and Confidence; in all moments."

"I resonate, emanate and am interconnected with all life in Joy, Love, Abundance, Freedom, Health, Success, Security, Companionship, Creativity, Peace, Life, Wholeness, Beauty, Enthusiasm, Contentment, Spirituality, Enlightenment and Confidence; in all moments."

This opportunity to free yourself is my gift to you. The gift that you can give yourself is to recognize its value and to take this technique seriously. Devotion to a true love is noble. But many of us have spiritually outgrown blind loyalty. It is important for everyone's empowerment to know the difference.

It can also benefit you to give this to your friends and family members who are dealing with a breakup. When they lament about another person, they are begging the Universe for help. This worksheet is the Universe answering their call through you.

214 SEE YOUR INTERACTIONS

See your interactions as a surrogate for the interactions of the multitudes. What you do as an individual is a role model for humanity even though they may never know of you. When you have even a small victory, it is a victory for all. You and what you do are that important.

215 HONING THE HO'OPONOPONO TECHNIQUE

There is a technique that helps people heal from all worldly issues by saying four specific statements to those that have been wronged. The premise is that everything in the world that you are aware of is directly related to you and if you apologize with these four statements, powerful healing occurs.

I AM SORRY

I LOVE YOU

PLEASE FORGIVE ME

THANK YOU

A very subtle tweak of this technique is to use it this way: Feel into something that brings you a feeling that is not desirable in the body. Think of how your body feels when you eat the wrong food. Feel how the body feels when you feel unworthy or not good enough. Hone into the thickest part of that feeling. Focus on it like a target.

As you hold your attention on that feeling, speak directly to that feeling. Say these four statements very sincerely to those feelings that you have "pinned down". Feel the energy of the issue untangle as palpably as if you were untying a knot. Because that is exactly what is happening.

216 TRANSCENDING

Any group that says it is the way to absolute truth is putting a cap on truth. It may be the purest way to truth and could be absolutely right. But at one point, the individual has to break away from the rocket and maintain orbit of their own accord. To prevent this natural progression from occurring is defeating the whole purpose of the rocket.

The rocket itself can't maintain the orbit that the individual has been catapulted to. The sheer bulk of its words and guidelines are enough to ground the individual. One can stay in the hull of the rocket out of fear of crashing and burning. Or, one can do the task that all its training has led to and trust in the process of transcending. It is done alone and unencumbered by doctrine.

This is the true test of Mastership. It is not about loyalty or allegiance to the process but a willingness to soar to new heights in new realms. It is to encourage others in their individuality to detach from all fear; to surrender all adornments to be enlightened and sustained in the reality of unconditional, perpetual and pristine divine love.

217 MASTERING DIRECT KNOWING

There is so much that we humans don't know. In the past, it was fine to conquer the world around us. It was a very big task. But because of an expansion of consciousness, that is not enough any more. The world has gotten smaller because our awareness of it has become bigger.

It is time to break free of the habitual complacency that mankind has been conditioned to accept. It is time now to wonder and stretch the mind and imagination past its current capacity. Did you know that any question you ask, the Universe it will give the answer?

Try it. Ask a question where you don't know the answer to the Universe and see how long it takes the Universe to answer. Start with mundane questions, and when you get a sense of the process, ask more elusive ones. You will be surprised at your own intelligence when you push the envelope by asking and having answered real, amazing things. This is what the inventors and innovators do. Can you imagine if we all operated this way?

218 VANTAGE POINT

When we gain an understanding of the dichotomy of the simplicity and complexity of life, we realize the adventure of every experience. Every situation can be looked at in a most complicated way, boiled down to a simple faction, or looked at through a myriad of gray scales.

The beauty of life is that we get to deal with it from any or every level that we wish. And the more conscious we are, the more we get to choose which level we wish to indulge in. Our experiences are the scenarios that we set up to develop our unique skill set. We can either create dramas, catastrophes or a paradise. It is all in our choice of vantage point.

219 LIVING YOUR PURPOSE

(Say each statement three times out loud while tapping on the top of your head at the crown chakra and say it a fourth time while tapping on your chest.)

"I release the fear of living my purpose; in all moments."

"I release allowing outer circumstances to interfere with me living my purpose; in all moments."

"I release being overwhelmed by the thought of living my purpose; in all moments."

"I release defining living my purpose with massive responsibility; in all moments."

"I release defining living my purpose as a burden; in all moments."

"I release allowing unworthiness to sabotage living my purpose; in all moments."

"I release all the confusion in figuring out what my purpose is; in all moments."

"I release allowing someone else to tell me what my purpose is; in all moments."

"I release losing touch with my purpose; in all moments."

"I make space in this world to live my purpose; in all moments."

"I remove all blockages to living my purpose; in all moments."

"I connect wholeheartedly in living my purpose; in all moments."

"I stretch my capacity to live my purpose; in all moments."

"I release any fear, doubt and hesitancy in living my purpose; in all moments."

"I now recognize how to live my purpose; in all moments."

"I am centered and empowered in living my purpose; in all moments."

"I resonate and emanate with living my purpose; in all moments."

220 YOU ARE THE CENTER OF YOUR WORLD

What is your purpose? You know of the greatness that walks within you. You have the willingness, strength, and the awareness to make a difference. You only need the tools, techniques and the confidence to step into this role.

Did you know that you are the only one holding you back from having that great life that you dream of? The spiritual laws that run the Universe are as exacting as the law of gravity. One such law is the Law of Abundance. It is everyone's birthright to live in abundance with Joy and Ease. If that is not your reality, it is because of your personal belief system...and YOU are the only one to change that.

You are a Healer. Energy flows fluidly through your being and animates your physical body. When you are healthy, the currents are flowing well. But when you overthink and stress your body with physical and emotional toxins, you dam up your own currents of life force and it may manifest as dis-ease in the body.

You are the Center of your World. You are the magnificent sun of your own cosmic Universe. Everything that comes into your sphere of influence is because you allowed it. The more attention you put on your own Divine Loving nature and its benevolent influence, the more you will generate uplifting experiences in your life. You are a creator.

221 HOW IT WORKS

When I help people with their physical, emotional, and mental pain, I do so by staying detached. What that means is I look at it from a vantage point that is not at the same "frequency" as the issue. Meaning, if it is emotional issues, I don't respond emotionally. If it is mental anguish, I don't hash it out with the client.

I look at it as energy and explain to people what the triggers are and what the issues are, how they are triggering their present life, and then I disconnect it and release it. To me, I feel it like congestion, like a stuffy room, and I dissipate it with my intention. Usually the client feels some evidence of a shift. They will feel lighter or be able to breathe deeper or have a sense of relief.

Love is a conduit. When one is in love with another, they are in the same "space." When I facilitate a session, I am in love with the client. That is why I am able to perceive what they are perceiving. If the client does not feel comfortable with me, they will close off and there is little sharing. In this way, they are always in control. Since love is the mainstay, I assist others only to the degree that they are able to trust the process. For many, just getting up the incentive to work with me is a catharsis. They may get anxious before a session because the stagnant energy that they have been suppressing may be coming to the surface to release.

After a session, the client will many times want to backtrack and talk about the issues. I will not allow it. It is a way of pulling it back to themselves. They also want to describe issues to me. Describing issues is a way to bring another person to the same level as your issues. It is an unconscious way to get relief by transferring one's issues. Please don't use people this way. Please learn a more detached way of dealing with your issues.

Technique: Whatever your discomfort, whether it is physical, emotional or mental agitation, sense it as a stagnant cloud of energy within you. Visualize moving it out of yourself like watching a cloud pass in the sky. Watch the cloud pass out of you and immediately see it dissipated into a river of light or the cleansing rays of sunshine. In this way, you will not be inflicting your issues on another being.

222 THE DYNAMICS

I open my heart to ease the pain of someone who is struggling. They feel better and are energetically uplifted. Then they see an opening and start talking about the negative that we just released. They pull it back and shove it into me. They aren't trying to bring me down, but that would be the result if I allowed it.

I know enough to pull away, release what they just shoved into me and close up my energy field as protection. Most times after that I will have to be on guard with them because they will try again and again to dump their issues. This dynamic plays out again and again.

I think it is funny that someone wouldn't allow a neighbor to bring all their garbage to their house and unload it on their lawn, but they will allow anybody to unload their emotional issues into their energy field and think it is okay.

This dynamic happens a billion times over every day. People have to be educated in their energetic responsibility towards others. We have to teach others how to treat us yet still have compassion for them when they struggle with this lesson. We can especially save others from dis-ease by not shoving our issues onto them.

223 RAISING OUR VIBRATION

There is a missing component in individuals manifesting abundance. It can happen, but there has to be a means of holding the vibration of anything we desire. When someone who has never had physical wealth comes into money, the first thing they do typically is spend it all. There is such a disconnect between depravity and abundance that people do not know how to hold the vibration of wealth in their energy field. They repel it when they get a chance to experience it.

This concept works in all matters. When someone loses a lot of weight, they have to learn to hold the vibration of a thin person or else they will binge and gain all the weight back really quickly. When there are makeover shows, they are helping the person hold beauty in their sound frequency. That is the purpose of college and trade schools: To infuse the vibration of a particular craft in one's sound frequency. It is very difficult to do it without assistance. It can be done by the self focusing on the desired results and thinking and imagining as much as possible on the desired results. But that is difficult to do if one has lost their passion.

If one has attained a higher vibration in a particular area, it is a noble cause to assist others in holding a similar vibration. That is the purpose in my intention of sharing so much of myself and so many techniques. My intention is to assist in raising the vibration of the planet to match the frequency of love. I believe if all the inhabitants of the world vibrated closer to Joy, Love, Abundance, Freedom and Wholeness, those attributes would be the norm instead of the exception to what we see reflected now.

Here is a shortcut to attaining and holding the vibration of a desired intention:

(Say each statement three times while tapping on your head and say it a fourth time while tapping on your chest.)

"I remove unhappiness from my sound frequency; in all moments."

"I infuse Joy into my Sound Frequency; in all moments."

"I resonate with Joy; in all moments."

"I remove hate from my sound frequency; in all moments."

"I infuse Love into my Sound Frequency; in all moments."

"I resonate with Love; in all moments."

"I remove poverty from my sound frequency; in all moments."

"I infuse Abundance into my Sound Frequency; in all moments."

"I resonate with Abundance; in all moments."

"I remove enslavement from my sound frequency; in all moments."

"I infuse Freedom into my Sound Frequency; in all moments."

"I resonate with Freedom; in all moments."

"I remove disease from my sound frequency; in all moments."

"I infuse Health into my Sound Frequency; in all moments."

"I resonate with Health; in all moments."

"I remove failure from my sound frequency; in all moments."

"I infuse Success into my Sound Frequency; in all moments."

"I resonate with Success; in all moments."

"I remove isolation from my sound frequency; in all moments."

"I infuse Companionship into my Sound Frequency; in all moments."

"I resonate with Companionship; in all moments."

"I remove conflict from my sound frequency; in all moments."

"I infuse Peace into my Sound Frequency; in all moments."

"I resonate with Peace; in all moments."

"I remove death/depression from my sound frequency; in all moments."

"I infuse Life into my Sound Frequency; in all moments."

"I resonate with Life; in all moments."

"I remove fragmentation from my sound frequency; in all moments."

"I infuse Wholeness into my Sound Frequency; in all moments."

"I resonate with Wholeness; in all moments."

224 TAPPING INTO YOUR OWN WISDOM

People oftentimes put too much importance on feelings when they are not a very sophisticated level of awareness. Think about it. Feelings are the most rudimentary way of gauging safety. When a baby has a need, it learns to cry as a means for survival. People who want to connect will laugh together even if it is at the expense of another. People lash out in anger which is sometimes very hard to control.

To validate being driven by feelings, people will defend the feelings with their thoughts. Thoughts are very subjective and can be broached from any angle. That is why different people can look at the same experience from different vantage points and have very different conclusions.

Some will act without thinking. Some will think without feeling. Some will be led by their emotions. All show a different way of missing the mark.

A wise person will check in with their emotions, thoughts and experiences before they act, meaning they will not do anything without gathering all the information from all the different aspects of themselves about any situation. This doesn't need to be a tedious process. It can take moments.

There are different sensory systems in the body that help us gauge what is right action for ourselves. There is one in the gut, one in the heart, and another near the solar plexus. They are gauges that tell us what our higher truth is. If we learn to listen to them, we save ourselves a lot of problems.

When making a decision, if one gets that knot in the stomach or chest, they know that choice is not best for their higher good. It is their own inside information. The more one listens to that twinge, the easier their life will be.

Test it out on simple things. Even use it to dress yourself. If an outfit feels uncomfortable in any way, then change. Then try it out on bigger decisions. It is the best tool that you can have at your disposal. It is tapping into your own wisdom.

225 HOW AWESOME IS THAT?

The molecules in inanimate objects are still living organisms. If you are mindful of this you will be creating more of a loving environment and even a more loving world. You would be changing humanity on a cellular level. How awesome is that?

226 HOW TO LIVE YOUR PURPOSE

This is a question that gets asked a lot. People make it more complicated than it needs to be. Your purpose isn't revealed by wondering about things like income or accolades. It is by stripping everything down to what you are compelled to do.

Usually, we have the raw materials around us to live our purpose. For example, someone who lives in a landlocked area would not easily be a sea captain. It can happen, but usually the Universe will be more realistic. Some of the greatest influences in sports, the arts and humanities were introduced to their craft at a very young age.

Here is some help. Remove the fear of failing. Remove the need to make a living. Take away all diminishing thoughts of unworthiness. Take away playing it safe or having a plan B. Evaporate all the wants and hopes of your parents or spouse. Ask yourself the following questions:

- What am I naturally good at?
- What am I compelled to do?
- What would I still do even if I were a millionaire?
- Who/what do I love?
- What would I be doing if I didn't care about what others thought?

Since living our purpose is such a dynamic concept, we make it overwhelming in our minds. It is, in actuality, as simple as doing what we love to do and doing it without fear or interference. The more we do what we love, the more the Universe will make it part of our mainstay. It will get to the point where our purpose is really about being in a loving center and pouring that out into the world on a continuous basis.

Here are some taps to assist:

(Say each statement three times while tapping on the top of your head and say it a fourth time while tapping on the chest.)

"I release the fear of living my purpose; in all moments."

"I release being derailed from living my purpose; in all moments."

"I release confusing living my purpose with accumulating money; in all moments."

"I release living the dream of someone else; in all moments."

"I make space in this world to live my purpose; in all moments."

"I remove all blockages to living my purpose; in all moments."

"I stretch my capacity to live in my purpose; in all moments."

"I am centered in living my purpose; in all moments."

227 THE PIPELINE TECHNIQUE

All the memories that you have ever had are pipelines to experiences that are still happening in the now. Everything is happening in the now. Instead of trying to wrap the mind around that, try envisioning that the you in the now is a hub that runs pipelines to all that you have ever experienced, regardless if you remember it or not.

Right now, in the moment, envision a perpetual floodgate of divine love pouring into you from every direction and angle. See the divine love saturating the you that you are now and also flooding into every one of those pipelines. Any experience that you remember of when you were sad, in need, helpless or feeling disconnected, see the love gushing through the pipeline of that experience. See it flooding the you that you were then with incredible divine love until that you is completely happy, healthy, content and whole.

Do this with every single pipeline. You don't have to remember each one to realize that you are saturating every other time and place. See the divine love saturate all the pipelines until you realize that you are bringing all those different experiences into the now with divine love. You are stretching your awareness of the now to encompass all of the other experiences until the now encompasses everything.

Expand your vantage point from the hub and stretch out your overview to include every single pipeline to every experience. If you want to, you can go back into any pipeline to you in pain and fix it by pouring the love into it. Learn to toggle between the hub, each pipeline and the overview of all. This exercise is developing you in ways that you will enjoy discovering on your own.

You are developing and experiencing your own omniscience, omnipresence and omnipotence.

228 GUARDIAN TECHNIQUE

(Say this statement three times while tapping the top of your head. Then say it a fourth time while tapping the center of your chest.)

"I stand guardian of all my thoughts and deeds so as to stay centered in and emanate my highest truth; in all moments."

It may create a solid feeling in your body right away.

229 TECHNIQUE TO HONE YOUR CRAFT

Whatever you are doing (yoga, dance, singing, studying or sleeping), visualize all the cells of your body doing it in sync with you. See every single cell as a mini-version of you. See all of them coordinating their efforts to assist you in overcoming the task at hand.

230 TECHNIQUE TO EXPAND YOUR ENERGY

We are actually in the fifth dimension but are operating as if we are still in the third dimension. This is difficult on us. It shows up as being overwhelmed and trying to hold everything together through shear will. Don't. Let go.

In contemplation, visualize all the cells of your body as flower buds. They are all contained and defined by their own space. Then visualize all the little buds blooming open and blending into each other. Feel the expansiveness of your energy in a powerful new way, gentle and strong. This is your new state of consciousness.

Once you have done this for yourself, do it for all the atoms outside of your body. See how you then blend with all of life. Feel how strong, yet fluid you are and how connected you are with all of life. You can feel empowered as you can spread your consciousness through all of life. Let love ebb and flow through you, and to and from you.

231 THE LAST GAME OF CANDY CRUSH

You know that feeling when you have been spending too much time on a level of Candy Crush. You are not enjoying the game anymore but can't seem to stop playing? Your eyes are blurry and you have definitely had enough? This is the brink that many people are at in their life. They are tired of the game and it isn't fun any more, but they keep playing out of compulsion.

Greed, judgment, gossip, and focusing on problems is a compulsion as well. It is up to each individual to decide that they have had enough and to simply walk away from them. Once they pull themselves away, it is easier to live without them. That is when love and freedom open up to the individual. They can take part in the awakening.

232 THE SUPER BOWL TECHNIQUE

It's not about the game. It is about so many people converging their attention into one single intention. It is a powerful energy. We are all watching the game individually, yet we are all doing it together. There is a palpable sense of everyone else watching the game as well.

So instead of focusing your attention single pointedly on what is transpiring on the screen of your TV, expand your energy to also be aware of every single person watching the game as well. You can get a sense of the partying, the disgruntled, the hyper children and you can embrace it all as you.

Pour your love into the whole group consciousness of those engaging in watching the game. Pour your love into even those who are aware of the game but are too disgruntled to watch. Pour your love into all those indifferent to the game. Stretch your capacity to love all of them with the love that you would usually reserve only for your dear ones. Pour it into every single being that you can embrace in their awareness of the game.

These moments of connection are priceless. Pour infinite love into them. This is the way we empower, inspire and uplift each other and all of humanity. It has never been about the win. It has always been about the connection.

233 THE CORRELATION BETWEEN HEALING AND PHYSICS

I asked my brother who is a genius at explaining complicated concepts to explain anti-matter to me. I am convinced that how I assist clients is based on physics and other physical laws. So I am trying to find a way to bridge an understanding from my work to mainstream thought.

I am not able to even articulate our conversation, but I know there is something relevant in what I do. He was talking about unknowns and invariables and that anti-matter is the mirror image of matter. And when a particle of matter is introduced to its mirror image, they turn into nothing and a huge amount of energy is released. (Please no physics lectures. I understand my rudimentary butchering of Einstein's work.)

He explained about some principle where there are two waves of energy--maybe electrical and magnetic--that are intertwined together. When he said this, it occurred to me that maybe thought energy is magnetic and emotional energy is electrical (or vice versa), and that matter is the literal manifestation of all thoughts and emotions.

Going with this theory, it occurred to me that I do use this principle when I am working with clients. What if there were two kinds of manifestations? What if everything is the product of an emotion supported by a thought or a thought supported by an emotion? For instance, say someone is sad and there is a reason or thought that supports the sadness. What if you introduced the mirror image of this to them and used it to just dissipate the whole issue? What if a positive thought supported by an emotion is similar to anti-matter and will destroy the original emotion? I have done this and it works.

The mirror image of a sadness supported by a weak thought is a strong thought supported by a positive emotion. When I used this technique, it surprises people and brings them right out of a funk. It seems that the byproduct is clarity.

Take a sad thought that someone lays on you. They are expecting you to add a sad thought to it like sympathy and make it even a heavier shroud for them to cocoon themselves in. For example, "My boyfriend broke up with me." The person is telling you this in anticipation of the sympathy they will accrue from sharing.

Instead of giving them sympathy, give them a strong thought supported by an emotion. Instead of saying "I am so sorry," which they believe is their right to hear, say something positive. For instance, "Well isn't that great that you are free of a situation that you knew wasn't going anywhere and you didn't have to hurt him. How awesome!" The person will be stunned into silence maybe. To their emotion that is supported by a thought, you introduced its mirror image, a thought supported by an emotion.

The important thing to realize is that your counter-thought MUST be true and MUST be supported by an emotion or else you have just offended them deeply. You could say the same thing to them, and if it isn't supported by a sincere emotion, then it will not have the effect planned.

Try this with any situation. The key is that the thought has to be true to your knowledge and it has to be supported by an emotion. If you have someone who always complains and tries to get attention for it, practice this technique on them and see if it doesn't free you of their barrage of negativity. For anything that they throw at you, there is a counter thought with emotion with which to dissipate it.

So here is the equation:

Negative emotion propped on a thought + Positive thought supported with emotion = Freedom.

Here are some examples:

"I am sad because my dog just died." Counter: "You have an angel always by your side now."

"The town was devastated by a hurricane!" Counter: "Isn't it amazing how people pull together in the time of crisis." (Remember the thought has to be supported by the emotion to work.)

"Life is just getting harder and harder." Counter: "People are becoming so strong from their experiences."

I am not certain if my physics theory is sound. I just know that I help people dissipate their issues in a relatively short time. I know it isn't magic. I know it isn't as far-fetched as people who don't understand the process may think. I know that I tune into people at a very profound level, and if they don't understand or are invested in their issues, they may fear the process. But people who I have helped realize the one simple truth: What I do is done out of Love and Love is a conduit for its success.

234 THE RIVER TECHNIQUE

Choose ten great souls that inspire you and why. Use them as a benchmark to what you too can attain. What one can do, another can do. Strive to surpass them all. Instead of thinking of greatness as an abstract concept, think of it as an attainable goal for all. Hold others to the highest standard as well.

1) Mr. Rogers: His kindness

2) Mother Theresa: Her service

3) Pope Francis: His capacity to love and inspire

4) Princess Di: Her likability

5) Michael Jackson: His talent

6) Oprah: Her influence

7) Martin Luther King: His work for equality

8) Gandhi: His method

9) Angelina Jolie: Her inner and outer beauty combined

10) Paul Newman: His giving back

(Please don't judge my list. It's my list.)

Great souls started out as average people who Loved, Gave, Worked and Dreamed outside of convention. There is a great soul inside every single one of us. Great souls don't look around to see what everyone else is doing. They live by higher standards, give in greater measures and love with a greater capacity.

Think of a person in your life who best reflects the qualities above back to you.

In Contemplation:

Visualize the ten people on your list not as people but as ten currents of water in a stream. They flow in and out of each other and intermingle. They combine their forces and create an effervescent, loving, powerful flow of energy while still maintaining their individuality. Now visualize yourself as a person wading into the river to swim. Start swimming with the current and visualizing yourself morphing into a current of the river as well. Sense the currents of the ten people both individually and combined (while still maintaining their individuality as well as your own), and yet interweaving with the others. Keep flowing until you sense the other currents falling away and you being the whole river.

Invite the person from your life to witness you in the river and encourage them to share their gifts and dive into their own river. (Never, never visualize more than inviting them.) Maybe share this technique with them. Feel the vibrancy of the river. Get a sense of other souls walking at the edge of it and being encouraged to use their gifts as well. (Don't visualize who they are. That is their business). Pan out until you see the river as wider and bigger and flowing past all the billions of people of the earth.

Feel the Joy, Love, Abundance, Freedom and Wholeness of the River. See it, see you flowing into the heart of Love, becoming lighter, more expansive and ever more pure. Feel more Love mixing into the River until you become Love itself. Be the River, be the Love. Be Love itself.

235 SPIRITUAL ACTIVISM – TECHNIQUE TO UNTANGLE THE WORLD

Think of the world as a big knotted up ball of yarn. It looks unmanageable. But every time you do something nice for someone, you are loving, kind or even just smile, you are pulling the end of the yarn through a knot to relieve the world of some of the entanglement. Imagine that whenever you are kind to others, you are aligned with millions of people and showing them how to be kind and loving as well.

You may never know them in this world, but you are the conduit for showing them how to untangle the ball with you. See all the wonderful people in the world as actively working to untangle the ball of yarn so that kindness and benevolence come to each heart with ease. Use your thought energy with a loving intention in your quiet corner of the world to bring about empowering changes to the world we live in.

By doing this continuously, you will be doing more good than any energy committed to activism. In fact, this is a form of spiritual activism. It is done without outing antagonists. Isn't that the more loving thing to do? It is converting all of the efforts into effectiveness without wasting any on division or self-righteousness.

Some people enjoy the outer banter. But for those of us who don't, we no longer have to feel guilty about not helping humanity. We can be efficient in assisting other souls and the world at large with this humble technique.

236 LET'S DISLODGE A LOGJAM

Think of yourself as a tube of energy. When you are tired, sick, or depressed, it is like the energy in the tube is sluggish or isn't moving. Anything you do of a positive nature can be seen as unjamming the tube. It doesn't have to be a big thing, and you may not know what will get your energy moving again. But you have to keep trying to dislodge your flow of energy. Everything you do of a positive nature is an attempt to flush your energy through.

When someone else is feeling down, showing them a simple kindness can be what is needed to unjam their energy flow. That is what is wrong with the world. It is suffering from one big logjam. We, with our kindness, awareness and intention, are capable of dislodging one big worldwide logjam.

237 PUT AN END TO THIS SELFISH ACT

I admonished another dear soul for their selfish shortcoming. It is the only flaw that is not acceptable. They refused a gesture of kindness from me. They do not realize how thoughtless an act that is. The whole Universe exists as fluid energy passing through all souls. The way to bring this beautiful synchronicity to a grinding halt is to refuse to receive. It is far more acceptable to refuse to give than to refuse to receive. It is far more damaging to refuse to receive.

When someone with a fluid energy gives, there is a force behind that. When it hits a wall, it is energetically damaging. It is similar to a fast moving car hitting a brick wall. That is what happens when one refuses to receive. The world is paralyzed in such actions. There are those of us working to untangle deep rooted knots by perpetual giving. The only kind thing to do is to allow this force to move unencumbered through the world by accepting the gifts that are presents.

Refusing to receive, on an energetic level, has been a tactical means of paralyzing energy and stopping the flow of love in the world. Please don't be a part of it. Please accept gifts when you can and do your part. The gifts perpetually abound. Please start receiving.

238 TECHNIQUE TO TURN CHAOS INTO CELESTIAL MUSIC

The frequency of Love is 528 Hz. There are recordings of it on the Internet. Create a CD of it. Play it in the background loud enough to hear it but low enough so it disappears in the background. Put it on continuous play. Remember what it sounds like as a single tone because if you are sensitive, it will change to the most beautiful music.

You may have to do a double take many times to remember that when you turned the CD player on, it was just a single tone. The music may elicit such reverence and peace of the most sacred holidays. The music will be rich and round and expansive. It may take several hours, but hopefully you will experience this. The pets and the environment will feel calmer and more harmonious.

This is a great way to bring harmony into the home because everyone's and everything's atoms will be resonating similarly. If there is noise from the neighborhood that is intrusive, notice how the music creates a buffer from it. You may also sense a positive cohesiveness in the space outside of your home as well.

I would love to hear people's positive experiences with it.

239 HOW TO SAVE THE WORLD

What if the world's destiny wasn't so much written in stone but was a compilation of the thoughts and actions of all its inhabitants? What if the perceived downfall of earth was merely a self–fulfilling prophecy? Do you think that things have taken a turn for the worse and the world doesn't seem too hopeful? Maybe all the negative advertising, war coverage and rhetoric is finally taking a toll on us. Maybe our personal thoughts and everyone's personal negative thoughts need to change. Maybe that is what will bring about hope for a better outcome for the world.

Many groups and individuals feel that they need to take up causes to save the world. It is good to pour passion into the world, but it doesn't have to be at the cost of another person's freedom. Meaning, your loving intent may be helpful, but not if it relies on everyone else to get on your bandwagon too.

Here is an example. Many people want you to wear a pink ribbon or fight for a cure to a disease. If you do not comply, they think you are not sympathetic. This is social peer pressure. I empathize with those who have lost loved ones to an illness. But the cure is right in front of us and society doesn't want to do the hard work, so they distract themselves with races and causes that don't address the issue. It is group denial.

So many diseases are caused by contaminated water, food and air. It is not rocket science. But people have been bullied by institutions that say that everything is safe and well. But those of us who have common sense realize that all the pink ribbons and all the research in the world isn't going to change the quality of air and water. (Where does the research money go that people use all their heart and lifeblood to raise? Back into big business in the form of research.)

The world is full of noble causes to rally around. But when one puts their attention on the problem, they are giving it attention and making more space for un-resolve in the world. Those who protest for peace find themselves in the center of conflict. Those who take up animal rights squabble on different sides of the same issue with fellow animal lovers.

What if the real way to resolve conflict in the world was to resolve conflict within ourselves? What if all the pettiness in our lives, the half-truths and denial were taken care of within ourselves and we supported others to do the same. What if it didn't matter how someone processed love for community, God, family and country? What if it all boils down to love and commitment within ourselves? Whatever that looks like, we can better ourselves without trying to persuade others to see life from our vantage point.

240 SHATTER THE GLASS CEILING TECHNIQUE

There are limitations that are put on certain demographics in the world. These are called glass ceilings. In America, there is a phrase in business called shattering the glass ceiling. It means breaking through these invisible limitations that everyone is aware of but are not really acknowledged openly. The example of men making more money for the same job as women is a glass ceiling.

There are so many glass ceilings in the world based on race, gender, skin tone, religion, species, social and economic status and spiritual beliefs that it doesn't feel like it is a fair place to live. Some people seem to benefit from all the advantages. But something that is not based on outer conditions is our ability to perceive and be aware of our own subtle empowerment. Those who may seem helpless in having any status in the outer world can be rich in spiritual awareness and their ability to move all of humanity to a kinder, more loving existence.

In contemplation, see the earth from the vantage point of it being small enough to maneuver around. As you look at it, you squint and see that the atmosphere around it is not clear. There are layers and layers of glass ceilings that encased it. Some are really thick. They could represent a universal glass ceiling of women's rights around the world. Some are more subtle. Some glass ceilings are little bubbles over different parts of the world. They can represent anything like lack of education or religious persecution.

Suddenly, you notice that there is a durable mallet near by. You pick up the mallet and start shattering all the glass ceilings on earth. As you do, you notice your own lung capacity seems deeper and you feel more comfortable in your skin. There are some that are thicker and some that shatter really easily. But as they do, the glass seems to just turn to fine powder and dissipate.

Whenever you get a sense of a limitation put on anyone, just go back to this technique and shatter the ceilings. It is important to do this in a detached way without targeting anyone in specific. You are not out for revenge. You are just balancing an outmoded wrong. Shatter all the limitations. When you are finished, you should see the earth free and unencumbered.

This new world is the one many of us want to be on. Maybe you will notice some of us helping take down the limitations. Perhaps it is what we have come here to do.

241 THE POWER OF INTENTION

I went to visit my friend who started a new job at a car wash. I wanted to support him and encourage him. When he finished wiping down my car Sparky, I gave him a ten dollar tip.

He told me after that he received many great tips, and it continued in the following days. That is the purpose of an intention. It is a magnetic force that primes the pump for more of the same.

So many success stories have the plot line of having one person believe in the main character when all others overlooked them. Who are we all overlooking? Is there someone out there you can encourage and be their motivation? We pay people to be our coaches these days. That is how important it is!

Inspire others to greatness and it will undoubtedly lead to your own!

242 WORKING WITH THE SPIRITUAL LAW OF INTENTION

There is a phenomenon that I have observed that would benefit others to be privy to. It is so subtle, it may have been missed as to how it works in our lives, yet it is vital to our own healing and wellbeing. It has to do with the incredible healing power of intention.

I have noticed that when one of my animals has a health issue to be dealt with, merely addressing it with an action heals the situation. Every single time I have taken one of my fur babies to the vet, their health issue clears up on the drive over to the office. One time, Simha had an issue where she was not eliminating for a couple of days. As soon as we got to the vet's office, she eliminated two days of waste in their front hedge. She was then fine.

I have watched this happen in many different areas of my life. It is an exacting spiritual law as prevalent and consistent as gravity. It is this. Using a pure intention to address an issue moves that situation to a resolve. Intention is a means of piercing the stagnant state of apathy and stirring movement into it so it can resolve. Thinking of any issue that is not moving in a positive way and infusing a pure intention into it is like unplugging a drain and watching the dross empty out and a clarity remain. This is spiritual law.

We are observing it on a grand scale in our political system. Our political system has been immersed in apathy. It is common to hear things like, "Why bother, nothing will change," or "Everyone is in it for themselves," etc. That is why voter turnout has been so low.

But now there are candidates that are not professional candidates. They have infused a greater intention into the process of politics. Whichever candidate that you choose, Bernie Sanders or Trump, they have both gotten the apathetic state of the government pierced with their pure intention. Both are playing a vital role in moving the country out of a state of apathy. We are seeing this reflected in an enthusiasm for the process that was not there before. That is why, even as flawed as Trump may be, he is still likable to so many. They are innately appreciating his intention.

Other ways that apathy shows up in our life is in our finances, health, career and diet. You can tell when someone is in that apathetic state by their self talk. They lament about never being able to make enough money, get healthy, get a job they like or lose weight. The apathy uses mental imagery of all their experiences of seeming to fail to keep them immersed in a stagnant state of non-action.

What people may not realize is that the Universe is conspiring with you in whatever your desires are. It is matching your intention and magnifying it. If you are too tired to attempt to change your circumstance, the Universe will match that intention as well. It will provide the fertile environment for you to continue in that apathetic state. The Universe does not judge your intentions. It merely magnifies the ones that you emit. Not making any choices is a powerful form of choosing, as well.

There have been so many times when I have tried to introduce a higher intention to someone who comes to me for help. It has amazed me how ruthlessly a person will defend their apathetic state. I have learned to cautiously introduce a positive intention to someone with fibromyalgia. Many will vehemently defend their pain.

Whenever I have introduced the intention of releasing the emotional issues that are driving the physical pain, I have met such resistance. In the instances that I have been privy to, I have seen that these people need a break from society. The pain gives them a reprieve from having to be part of a competitive community and affords them the reason to bow out and take care of themselves. Only some are ready to energetically address the issue. The emotional pain and abuse of someone that has fibromyalgia is so prevalent that the physical pain is the validation that they need to self-care.

Being aware of this spiritual law can be the means of addressing apathy in our own lives in so many ways. Think of the issue of dieting. Instead of worrying about what diet is going to work, focus on always poking through the apathy of adding a pure intention to the situation. People will start a regime and when it doesn't work, they return to a state of apathy. Instead of focusing on the details of the diet, change up the pure intention that is introduced.

That is why professionals say that diet and exercise work in unison to lose weight. It is introducing two intentions at once. How about instead of just hitting the situation of needing to lose weight with two intentions, you bombard it with multiple intentions that have less to do with losing weight (to move away from the apathetic state) and more to do with creating energetic movement in the system to unplug the drain.

Here are a few:

- Simply cut down on fats to benefit the heart.
- Cut down on sugar to help the blood sugar stabilize.
- Cut out everything white from the body--it creates an inner slime.
- Do activities that you love to bring more joy to your life.
- Put more attention on your appearance to feel good about yourself.
- Walk every day as a means to balance your mood.
- Commune with nature in the form of gardening or hiking.
- Connect with positive people to assimilate positive energy.

- Give up cursing or self-disparaging talk.
- Get professional counseling or coaching to access experts.
- Give up negative talk as it affects your vibratory rate.
- Volunteer in some way to feel good about yourself and to be grateful.
- Do the taps on my page to strip off layers of issues.
- Pray, meditate or commune with nature to plug into your omniscience.
- Encourage others--it is the quickest way to encourage yourself.
- See the best in others as it is the best way to see the best in yourself.
- Challenge every situation as an opportunity to pierce apathy and unplug a drain.

This is the shortlist of ways to address weight loss without making it about a number on a scale. Just looking for a number on a scale to move is a form of apathy in itself. With every situation in your life that is not moving, there is a means to address it with a similar list.

Also, we are addressing systemic apathy as a nation by supporting a positive movement introduced with a pure intention. There are two candidates that do this. Both are scoffed at by the media and their peers because the media and their peers are comfortable with and benefit from the systemic apathy. But if you try to imagine the potential of what we are not currently reaching with the current system, you can flip your vantage point by looking at it. You can move from seeing the non-candidates as naive to seeing the more career candidates as ignorant.

243 MERRY CHRISTMAS RIGHT NOW

What if Christmas was truly a state of heart that we could access at any time? What if Christmas was simply about emulating the kindness of an enlightened soul and the total opposite of drawing lines in the sand? What if it doesn't happen once a year but happens every moment? What would be the point of gifts, decorations and music except to convey that feeling to others?

What if Christmas could be experienced in a much simpler way? What if each kindness was sharing the Christmas Spirit? What if each smile did the same? Why can't it? Why not? Here's me saying Merry Christmas right now.

244 TECHNIQUE TO EXPAND YOUR CONSCIOUSNESS

In contemplation, think of yourself not as solid matter but as a compilation of atoms. Just a huge collection of atoms that came into agreement for you to have an experience of being a separate unit.

Visualize each one of those atoms as an inverted pillow that needs to be turned out to "fluff up" and to expand. Think of the inverted pillows as a defense that was once adopted the way a turtle will pull in its shell for safety. Get a sense of how all of the outward pain and confusion during wars and power plays caused the atoms to recoil.

But now it is safe. With your intention, visualize all the atoms expanding out to their natural state, like pillows being unfurled and expanded. Feel the expansion that intention brings. Scan your whole beingness to make certain that ALL the atoms are turned out. If you have had issues or pain in certain parts of your makeup, send your attention there to unfurl all the atoms. If you have struggled with depression, stubbornness or being over-analytical, send your intention to the head and the area around the head to open up all those atoms as well.

Know that each atom is still contained in its protective layer and you are still an embodiment of the collective of all of them. Just feel how expanded you are in your awareness and the residual benefits of this technique.

When you have gotten comfortable with the pillow analogy, realize and visualize each atom being a solar system of itself and each one happening within your awareness. Feel where that expansion takes you. You are always safe in your container of self, but get a sense how this expansion of consciousness benefits you. Within these atoms are held the answers to any question you could possibly ask.

The question becomes then, "Why are you playing it so small?" Realize that the solar systems within your atoms overlap the solar systems in everyone else. This is the way we are all connected.

245 KNOCK FIRST!

At some point, you are going to have to decide whether you are going to be nice and polite and let everyone come and go into your home at will, or if you will honor yourself by locking your own doors and windows and allowing only those who respect your home to enter.

What if they don't realize that you work diligently to keep your home clean? What if they have no idea what a clean home is supposed to look and feel like? What if they stop over all the time uninvited? What if they get offended when you ask them to use a coaster and take their muddy boots off before they sit on your white sofa? What if they spill and stain everything that you have collected to bring you a sense of wellbeing and comfort? What if they have no idea what they are doing? Would you allow it? If so, how long?

What if they are hoarders? What if they have so filled up their house that they need a place to bring more stuff? What if they collect items from around the neighborhood and just start bringing all their junk into your house taking over room after room after room? Are you going to be nice?

What if they have never lifted a finger to clean their own home? Does it matter? What if everyone just comes and goes in everyone's home in the neighborhood and it is the accepted norm? Are you going to join in?

This is what plays out many times a day with our own state of wellbeing. Your state of consciousness is your home. And all who tread in it should respect and honor your boundaries. Their lack of caring, awareness, abilities to respect it are not your concern. When are you going to stop being polite? When are you going to stop listening to every problem that people bring to you? When are you going to lock your own doors? When are you going to respect you own level of emotional and psychological hygiene?

When are you going to stop being flattered that people want to come in? Of course they do. You are a wonderful host. But it makes more energetic sense to teach others how to knock before they come in and to use the coaster. A pristine state of wellbeing is priceless, and if once in a while you have to shut the door, give yourself that guilt-free permission. Sometimes it is a necessary step in self care.

246 TECHNIQUE TO HEAL THE WORLD

If there is someone you work with, a relative or neighbor you don't get along with, go out of your way to do something kind for them. Break down the walls of resistance between you and them. Perform a kindness for them or give them a gift with no strings attached that will open their heart a bit. But be sure to do it with no expectation of receiving one ounce of appreciation in return. Do it so that you can show them what unconditional love looks and feels like.

If you have resistance to doing this, it is all the more reason to do it. It is not to win them over or to try to change them. It is to open yourself up to that feeling of being vulnerable to love and to melt your own scars and battle wounds. Whatever they receive from the exchange is personal to them and not your concern. Do it for yourself, and do it as a gesture to add more love into the world.

If we can't let go of the resistance in our own lives and attract more love to ourselves, how can we possibly expect to see a change in the world at large. The world is a reflection of our own lives. May it reflect true humanity, compassion and love.

247 TECHNIQUE TO LOVE YOURSELF

Everyone and everything is an aspect of ourselves. So when you are loving your child or a pet or you are gardening, think of everything that you engage as an aspect of you. See it as a mini-version of you. That love is the conduit of connection that needs to be encouraged in awakening humanity. So when you are showing a kindness to someone, change vantage points and see it as engaging yourself.

Then notice how you feel an aversion to being so loving to them. Work through the resistance to loving them as a version of yourself because that lack of self-love is what is holding humanity back from fluidly embracing. This is the block that is showing up in all your dynamics. When you have mastered loving yourself through everyone else, you will have an understanding of the inner connection of love that we all share.

You will realize how being taught to feel humble and unworthy was used for so long to prevent us from realizing the greatest truth. That we are all connected to Source and all are one.

248 PERPETUATING POSITIVITY

On the surface, consistently positive people seem weak. But it's much more difficult to be positive than negative. It takes much more discipline, authenticity and effort than following the flow of gossip and backbiting. Practicing the art of perpetuating positivity is a great way to live with purpose and integrity.

When talking to others, it's easier to feel a sense of belonging by trashing everyone and everything. This negativity seems to take on a life of its own. One simple, unflattering statement about another person or situation seems to be the hole in the damn that gushes forth a stream of negativity. How easy it is to start complaining about current events as a common ground. But as difficult as it is to abstain from negative comments, it's easier than trying to stop yourself once you start.

To hone your character, try lovingly countering a negative subject matter with a positive point about the same subject. See how it feels to inject positivity rather than negativity. It may surprise you how exhilarating it feels to break free from the negative stream with a simple positive or neutral statement.

If you don't want to participate in gossip without being confrontational, just don't respond. Just give a very short polite response to the person. A way to perpetuate positivity is by using positive reinforcement. Reward uplifting statements by engaging in conversation with the perpetrator. If conversation turns negative, politely excuse yourself. Realize that it's not about judging; it's about how the words make you feel. Judging is a negative behavior. Be loving and kind without being pious or playing the blame game.

Also pay attention to your own words and thoughts. You can consciously live your purpose only if you are clear of the muddy waters of negativity that try to keep you blinded to your truth. Faulting others is another illusionary way to feel superior. The reality is that it reveals your own character flaws.

Take a moment and read these words and see how they make you feel: hate, depression, illness, fighting, death, sadness, blame.

Now read these words: Joy, Health, Happiness, Laughter, Love, Fun, Freedom.

Words have a vibration and influence your mood and the mood of the environment. Choose to be happy by surrounding yourself with positive words and people. Feel the vibration of uplifting words resonate within you like music.

Be a leader. Pull yourself out of the muck of a negative thought stream and be the influence to pull those around you out as well. You will resonate with happiness and draw happiness to you. It takes a lot of character, and if done consistently, will bring you into peace.

249 LOVING BALANCE

In our natural state, our energy is perpetually flowing love. There is a desire, almost a compulsion, to give and share. We hold a memory of this complete loving within our energy field and it is that to which we aspire to return.

Due to trauma and fear, our loving flow diminishes to a trickle. Our access to the energy that fuels and inspires us diminishes. We shut down to a large extent and become less effective at helping ourselves and uplifting others.

Those who are trying hard to become effective again may become misguided in their sharing. They may try their best, but often their sharing becomes verbal rants or emotional dumping. Since their energy flow is still introverted, their sharing is based on fear or problems.

When someone is in this mode of processing, try to listen to them obliquely (if you feel you must listen at all). Sympathy has a low frequency, so giving too much sympathy can actually hinder someone more than help them. A better way to help is to validate their greatness rather than their issues. Remind them of their resilient spirit and that anything they are experiencing is temporary. They may try to bring you into their pain, but that is only out of fear or loneliness. They don't understand what they do.

To get out of that state ourselves, the best thing we can do is just give. Give of our talents, our time, our gifts in any way that allows us to prime the pump of generosity and love that is our natural state. But in doing so, realize that we have to include loving ourselves. Because when we can love others and love ourselves, then we are in balance.

250 JEN'S VERSION OF HO'OPONOPONO

Say these three statements silently to every soul you encounter, pass or that comes to mind:

"I LOVE YOU"

"YOU MATTER"

"YOU'RE PERFECT"

251 THE PEANUT BRITTLE TECHNIQUE

Power, self-interest, hate, fear and greed have kept factions glued together with a very strong bond. Weak people feel empowered by the negative bond they have with others. This turns individuals with little effectiveness into dangerous uncaring monsters doing real damage to individuals and humanity as a whole.

See these pathetic puny people being propped up by the stronger people in agreement with them and the negative stance they share. They are like puny peanuts held in their rigid stance by the group consensus. It happens in hate groups, corrupt government factions and in other settings like the mean girls in school.

Visualize these groups as peanut brittle. Simply imagine taking a huge mallet and smashing up all the brittle, which is hate and the psychic energy of the group. You do nothing to harm the peanuts which are individuals. You are merely breaking up the brittle that has condensed in society and has become a force to wreak havoc on humanity.

Feel how good it feels to break up the psychic energy that is trying to enslave humanity and diminish the empowerment of individuals. Watch the shifts ensue as we adopt this exercise and do it together. Remember that it is not possible to break up noble intentions. They are not brittle. It is also not possible to use this technique for anything other than to break up the hate and control. So enjoy freeing the peanuts.

252 THE EXTENSION OF YOUR OWN FACE

When I worked extensively with dogs, I realized how attached they were to their collars. When their owner would drop them off to be bathed, it was obvious that the collar was their connection to their human. They would get anxious when their collar was removed. It made them feel that they were losing their connection to their human. It was their security and connection to their life.

As I took off their collar, I would praise it no matter how tattered it was. I would reassure them that their human loved them and how special they were because they had a beautiful collar that was given to them. The whole point was to reassure them that they were not going to have to give up their collar, that they were only being separated from it temporarily, and being free of the collar did not mean that they were abandoned. They were still loved and safe regardless of whether or not they were wearing their collar.

This is a similar dynamic that I see people experience in relationship to their persona. They identify so strongly with their image and presence that they want to be reassured over and over that it is a good one. Having their image praised is their way of being reassured that they are loved, valued and safe. If people need to have their image or some aspect of themselves praised to feel validated, what is the harm in giving it to them? I see validating other people just as rewarding as validating the little dog who needed to be reassured that his owner was coming back to him. Why can't we do this for others?

It is because we were programmed to quantify ourselves in relationship to others in a pecking order. We were taught that if we rated someone else with positive traits, we were also rating ourselves in relationship to them and maybe it would mean we had a lower status. This is the lie and limitation of linear thinking.

In actuality, we are seeing our own traits mirrored for us in others. More people have an understanding that this is true. What this means is that if someone goes around proclaiming others as unattractive, undesirable, or being catty towards others in any way, it actually reveals an ugliness in the person making such observations. One who sees beauty and goodness in others is revealing their own beauty and goodness. Practicing this simple awareness could create an evolution of blossoming individuality.

There is no need to diminish anyone's collar. It is so much more admirable to secure the confidence of others with your words and thoughts. Just think of others as an extension of your own face. In doing that, you will be transcending archaic programming and will be promoting a huge healing shift in consciousness within yourself and others. You are the beauty that you see in others. Seeing beauty in others is finding it within yourself.

253 ENERGETIC LIPOSUCTION

To streamline a certain part of the body, a straw-like instrument will be inserted into the area to suck out the fat. The fat is a carrying case for an emotional issue. If you have trouble losing weight, perhaps it is the emotional issue that you need to release. Perhaps if you release the emotional issue, the fat will have no purpose and will leave as well.

Visualize inserting a liposuction tube into your body and sucking out the emotional issue that is being carried by a fat cell. Imagine sucking out all the issues and trauma out of your body through this tube and imagine it being sent into a processing system where it is recycled back into pure love. All things return to love at one point. See if you feel lighter and freer.

Use this issue if you are having pain in any one area or discomfort of any kind. There are many different uses for this technique that you may discover on your own. But think of more subtle issues like shyness or sexual inhibition being addressed using this technique.

254 HUMANS ARE LIVING, BREATHING PORTAL MAKERS

Anything humans put their attention on and fixate on, especially with passion (igniting the heart to work with the mind), will manifest. The problem is that humans have been subjugated and taught to manifest only negative scenarios for themselves and the world they live in, by default.

Every time you agree with a negative scenario, you are adding your portal-making abilities to that of another. You are fortifying a negative portal for yourself and others to walk through and exist in. Children innately understand this, and this is why they react so vehemently to the rules put on them by adults.

Creating negative portals has become so ingrained that people can't help thinking negative thoughts and scenarios. The thoughts come in at an alarming rate for some. It is distressing for someone who consciously tries to be positive to have these negative thoughts come through.

It is because they are trying to be positive that the negativity will inundate them more. It is no different from cold air rushing to meet hot air or vice versa and creating condensation. Here is a way to deal with negative thoughts that rush in and seem overwhelming.

Imagine a thought as a bubble forming as a new reality. It is emerging from your mind to manifest as a reality. With a conscious intention, simply pull the thought away from your mind before it is fully formed. Do this as many times as you have negative thoughts. Some people will have to keep at it diligently for a while. But eventually, you will learn not to waste your efforts creating negative scenarios because the conscious you will simply deflate them and watch them dissipate. Make this your new habit.

This technique has an added advantage. The you that is pulling off the negative reality is the you of higher consciousness. You will actually be adopting the vantage point of your higher self. It is a fast track to raising your consciousness.

255 CONSCIOUS CHOICE

What if with everyone we connect, we give or receive something? What are we giving out to others? What are we taking away from each encounter? How many times do we receive something undesirable and pass it off to the next person we encounter? How conscious do we choose to be?

If we go into every scenario, situation and even light encounter with the intention of giving only positive energy to others and choosing not to accept anything that is not beneficial, then we change the dynamics on all our interactions. In this way, we may uplift not only our lives, but all those we encounter.

256 THE SOCIAL MEDIA TECHNIQUE

See social media and all the people plugged into it as low level dust that kicks around like a dust storm. But it is not the people who are the dust. It is the negativity that they stir up. It is not they who are negative. They are merely carriers of this low level psychic energy that is intended to disturb our calm and choke out truth. They are being used as pawns by their willingness to use social media sites.

Social media and the technology was gifted to humanity by a superior race of beings to assist the earth in transcending out of primal mode. Primal mode consists of being interested in protecting self-interests and one's immediate loved ones with ill regard for others. It keeps people in the knee-jerk reaction of "us versus them" mode. It is what fixates people on war and on accruing mass amounts of stuff at the expense of the ecosystem. It is fascinated by violence and demonizes people and concepts of a higher vibration.

Earth was trapped in primal mode. It was a conscious decision by higher beings to assist us in transcending being nothing more that reactionary beasts. They incarnated in human form and brought forth the technology to allow us to interact with each other. They assumed that if we got to connect with people all over the world, we would see the commonality we all share and awaken to higher aspects of ourselves. Some are.

But the psychic energies of negativity that thrive off of man's lowest base nature have been using social media as a ploy to entrench people deeper into hate and division. Where the connection was intended to be used to allow people to meet heart to heart as a means to awaken humanity, it has been used as a ploy to train some to ruthlessly attack others with little thought of their own cruelty.

It has given a cover and a means for people to do incredible damage to other's psyche through training them to be psychic attack dogs through their computer. Someone could be harmless and kind in their real life, but unleash unlimited anger and ruthlessness on others that is matched only by their desperate need to matter and be heard. That is what we are witnessing in social media right now.

The negativity that ensues is not a random issue. It has not happened without incredible assistance from negative forces. It is intentional. We are merely pawns to a greater intention of keeping humanity enslaved to primal mode. In primal mode, they defend guns, crude oil, gutting the earth, synthesizing our food sources, dehumanizing our way of life and having us procreate as a mindless, ignorant means of perpetuating their agenda. The agenda to keep us enslaved to buying their guns, fighting their wars, breeding their soldiers, buying their products, swallowing their indoctrination and perpetuating their hate.

I have been tapping into direct truth and sharing it on social media as much as humanly possible. Those who have counseled me have told me to hold back what I write and only sell it to consumers in book form. But my Spiritual Guides have told me to share everything that I can as much as possible and pour truth out there. What I share is not opinion or based on the research of someone else. It is a direct connection to direct knowing. There are a couple of reasons why I was instructed to share so much and given access to greater truths.

The psychic energies that have dominated this world as an attempt to enslave all of humanity all but succeeded. But higher beings have stepped in to give humans a chance to awaken. The choice is to awaken or to perish in a fiery ball of their own hate. Many of us have awakened. Many of us are working diligently to assist all others to awaken. The vibration of truth was all but snuffed out of the resonance of earth.

What I share in words is actually seeding humanity with the vibration of higher consciousness. My writings are a lifeline to direct knowing for the reader. It is a means to show them that they too are capable of being conduits for incredible truth. They are the lifelines to all others and so are the seed bed of awakening humanity.

I have been thwarted on all sides. Technology gets sabotaged, people attack me, those who understand what I do here take offense easily and spend their days licking a wounded ego or stroking it in the protection of the false self. Every action of pure intention is thwarted, twisted, demonized and deflated. This is what humans have been trained to efficiently do. They will protect the ego at all costs. Even those who understand what I do here will distract me with petty grievances and seemingly benign affronts to my person. These are not small things. They are the last vestige to preventing a major shift in consciousness on the planet. They are calculated and ruthless energy that blows through as easily as the wind and uses whatever means it can to thwart the advancement of awakening.

I have no recourse but to persist. If everyone around me is too disheartened, too bored to read what I right, too scared to face themselves, so caught up in one incarnation to use their gifts to assist, I am still dedicated to the cause of awakening humanity. It is what I have come here to do. I do not feel the social joys that others experience. On paper, my life is pathetic to a fault. My insistence on relentlessly carrying on although all the tools at hand are limiting and perhaps ineffective, may seem pathological. Yet I will continue on because this is the course of where my talents lead me.

I have nothing else but the ability and the resilience to try to articulate a truth that has been hidden away in archives, bastardized, distorted, or used to enslave others. It is my continued intention to show people how to use their heart energy to overcome the mind directives that have been so jacked up with sabotages and booby traps. This is what I do in the techniques I share.

So use your visualization skills to get an overview of the earth. See all the negativity of social media as a low level dust storm that prevents individuals from connecting heart to heart. With a pure intention, visualize all the dust blowing away and dissipating. See this muddled energy dissipate and see all these piercing, white little energies all shimmering underneath all the confusion. Blow them clean with your intentions. See them shine brighter. Continue to do this until it no longer looks like a dust storm but a shimmering water reflecting the light and love of a greater light source. See what were grains of sand become pure perfect diamonds on a clear and pristine surface.

Do this as often as you can. Do this whenever you think of it. Before you get on your computer, do this technique and see how it enriches your communications. Do this as you start your day or before you go to work or run errands. See how the very room that you are in becomes brighter and note how much more pleasant your interactions are with others. Do this technique so often that it becomes attuned to your parasympathetic nervous system, meaning it becomes automatic. This is you going from helpless victim to empowered creator of the awakening of earth.

257 WHAT TO TELL YOURSELF

In quiet intimate moments of contemplation, here are healing things to tell yourself:

- Talk to your eyes and tell them that they're no longer responsible to release anguish through their tears.

- Tell them they never have to be burned by blinding winds or burning sun, or to be witness to horrendous atrocities again.

- Talk to your ears and tell them that they never have to be deafened by the cries of suffering again.

- Explain to your nose that it never has to be assaulted by the rotting acrid smell of putrid death. It will never let you down again by feeding such rotting assaults into your mouth.

- Tell your arms that they never have to raise up to strike down a life ever again.

- Tell your hands that they need never be used as weapons in battle again.

- Tell them that they need never grip any weapon that will take the life of another.

- Tell your beautiful cheeks that they never need to feel or express shame again with their demure blush.

- Tell your shoulders that they never have to carry the responsibility of the world on them again.

- Tell your hips that they no longer need to be twisted and gnarled by the guilt of all the times they rode you into battle.

- Tell your legs that they never again have to march towards death for a cause they don't believe in.

- Talk to your neck and tell it that it never has to be strung up or choked again as payment for a petty offense.

- Talk to your lips and tell them they never have to taste evil again.

- Tell you mouth that it never has to speak lies to survive ever again.

- Talk to your feet and tell them they never have to be ripped, torn or shredded in the journey again.

- Talk to your heart and tell it that it never has to be broken again. Remind it that no matter what it may perceive, it is healthy, whole, loved and appreciated.

- Talk to your stomach and tell it that it never has to be tortured with deprivation. If you don't send down food, it is merely to give it a rest.

- Tell your skin that it will never be burned off your body again because you spoke your truth.

- Talk to your beautiful form and tell it that it never has to be raped of its dignity again.

- Speak to your nervous system that it never has to endure unfathomable pain again.

- Talk to your essence and tell it that you will never be deceived into giving up your essence again.

Thank all aspects of you for their loyalty, service, integrity and strength. Validate each aspect of yourself and renew your commitment to it. Renew your commitment to you.

258 LEECHES AND SLUGS

Leeches and slugs have the same reaction to salt. Salt is so bad for them that if you have a leech attached to you, all you have to do is pour some salt on it and it will furl up into a harmless state.

So many good people are attacked by the people around them. They don't understand why. It is because truth creates a similar reaction to human leeches and slugs that salt has on their counterparts. Truth is toxic to these people. They will do anything they can to get away from the truth. They will stoop to a verbal assault and other unkindness to save themselves.

Even if you don't speak truth directly to leeches and slugs, the way you engage others creates an atmosphere of truth. To belittle and assault you is self preservation for them. It is not as personal as you think.

As a visual, imagine pouring granules of truth all over the world. Immerse the world in this truth. It is a way to dry up the leech and slug energy in humans.

259 I WISH

I wish you could see you through my eyes

To acknowledge the incredible beauty that you truly are

I wish you could drop the ugly layers of defenses

Or the habit to run away

I wish you would let go of all pretenses that kept you safe so many lifetimes

Know all enemies as merely friends with their own set of defenses

I wish you would stop clinging to problems and pain

Hooking them to yourself with the possessive word "my"

I wish you could let go of the fear that is obliquely fed to you by others

And habitually tapped into your veins, wean yourself off it

Forgo the drama of elusive illusion blowing around in the mind and settling in the heart

Break through the sac of false pride

Bash through to the Love and allow it to gush free

Searing through the shackles that have stained your grace

Relax in being un-shelled

Accept the raw skin feeling of the unencumbered you

Gather up the love from within and wrap yourself in its depth

Throw it over your head so that you can see yourself with Love's eyes

Feel the Love with Love's heart

Know yourself with Love's mind

And dissolve all dregs of separation.

260 EVERYTHING MATTERS

Everything is energy work. Everything matters. Everything deserves attention and reverence. If you can show reverence doing the most mundane or unpleasant task, you are good the rest of the time. Showing reverence when you are doing something unpleasant resets your inner compass to love and respect for all life.

ABOUT THE AUTHOR

Jen Ward, LMT, is a Reiki Master, Shaman, medical intuitive, gifted healer, and an innovator of healing practices. She is at the leading edge of energy work providing an upgrade of understanding of healing from the Third Dimension to the Fifth. She takes the mystery out of what is called faith healing by explaining the physiology behind it in common language. Faith healing is not magic or super powers but merely a heart-centered intention manifesting its capabilities. Jen says that there is nothing that a pure intention fueled by a loving heart cannot accomplish.

Humans are so conditioned to come from their mind and this creates the limitations on their abilities. The heart has no limits. Jen explains in the Fifth Dimension, we are all whole but we have brought with us our engrams (ingrained conditioning) from the Third Dimension. It is relatively easy for people to release their issues because in the Fifth Dimension, they are already whole. The work that Jen does is in empowering the individual to realize what they are truly capable of.

Jen is considered a sangoma, a traditional African Shaman, who channels ancestors, emoting sounds and vocalizations in ceremonies. An interesting prerequisite to being a sangoma is to have survived the brink of death. When Jen was first approached with the knowledge of being a sangoma, she had not yet fulfilled this prerequisite. However, in April several years ago, when she came back to society on the brink of starvation as a result of traumatic involuntary imprisonment, the qualification had been met. She returned to the world of humanity a devout soul inspired to serve.

Her special abilities have also allowed her to innovate a revolutionary technique for finding lost pets by performing an emotional release on the animal. Using this method, she has successfully reunited many lost pets with their owners.

Jen currently works as a long-distance emotional release facilitator, public speaker, and consultant. Her special modality encompasses a holistic overview of her clients from all vantage points, including their physical, emotional, causal, and mental areas, ultimately benefiting their work, home, family, and especially spiritual lives.

You can find Jen here:

www.jenward.com/blog

Twitter: @jenuinehealing

Facebook: Facebook.com/JenuineHealingwithJenWard/

OTHER BOOKS BY JEN WARD

Enlightenment Unveiled: Expound into Empowerment. This book contains case studies to help you peel away the layers to your own empowerment using the tapping technique.

Grow Where You Are Planted: Quotes for an Enlightened "Jeneration." Inspirational quotes that are seeds to shift your consciousness into greater awareness.

Perpetual Calendar: Daily Exercises to Maintain Balance and Harmony in Your Health, Relationships and the Entire World. 369 days of powerful taps to use as a daily grounding practice for those who find meditation difficult.

Children of the Universe. Passionate prose to lead the reader lovingly into expanded consciousness.

Letters of Accord: Assigning Words to Unspoken Truth. Truths that the Ancient Ones want you to know to redirect your life and humanity back into empowerment.

The Do What You Love Diet: Finally, Finally, Finally Feel Good in Your Own Skin. Revolutionary approach to regaining fitness by tackling primal imbalances in relationship to food.

Emerging From the Mist: Awakening the Balance of Female Empowerment in the World. Release all the issues that prevent someone from embracing their female empowerment.

Affinity for All Life: Valuing Your Relationship with All Species. This book is a means to strengthen and affirm your relationship with the animal kingdom.

The Wisdom of the Trees. If one is struggling for purpose, they can find love, and truth by tuning into the Wisdom of the Trees.

Chronicles of Truth. Truth has been buried away for way too long. Here is a means to discover the truth that lies dormant within yourself.

Collecting Everyday Miracles: Commit to Being Empowered. This book is a thought provoking means to recreate the moment of conception with everyday miracles. It is through gratitude and awareness. This is what this book fosters.

Healing Your Relationships. This book is a means to open up communications and responsiveness to others so that clarity and respect can flourish again in society.

All of Jen's books are available on her website: http://www.jenward.com/jens-books/

www.ingramcontent.com/pod-product-compliance
Lightning Source LLC
Chambersburg PA
CBHW060454090426
42735CB00011B/1985